GATHERING CARRAGEEN

Monica Connell

SANDSTONEPRESS
HIGHLAND | SCOTLAND

First published in Great Britain
and the United States of America by
Sandstone Press Ltd
Dochcarty Road
Dingwall
Ross-shire
IV15 9UG
Scotland.

www.sandstonepress.com

Editor: Moira Forsyth

The publisher acknowledges support from Creative Scotland
towards publication of this volume.

ISBN: 978-1-910124-46-8
ISBNe: 978-1-910124-47-5

Jacket design by Jason Anscomb
Typeset by Iolaire Typesetting, Newtonmore.
Printed and bound by Totem, Poland

For my father, Kenneth Connell,
and my friends in Donegal,
with love and gratitude

'All of us have a landscape of the soul, places whose contours and resonances are etched into us and haunt us. If we ever became ghosts, these are the places to which we would return.' Colm Toíbín, *A Guest at the Feast*.

Carrageen (*Chrondus crispus*) is a short, tufted, reddish brown seaweed that grows abundantly on the rocky shores of the Atlantic. In Ireland it is also known as Irish moss, carrageen moss or, in Irish, *carraigín*. It is used internationally in cosmetics and in the food and drinks industry as a stabiliser and emulsifier. In Ireland it is often boiled with milk to make a blancmange-like pudding called Irish moss: it is also traditionally believed to ease colds, flu and respiratory diseases.

CONTENTS

AUTHOR'S NOTE

In order to protect the identity of the people in Donegal who so generously shared their lives with me I have not mentioned the name of the village where Mark and I lived. Similarly, with the exception of one or two people who chose to be recognized, I have used pseudonyms.

HOMELAND

My sister and I are standing at the water's edge, the frayed residue of waves foaming around our bare feet. Behind us dry sand is blowing horizontally across the beach; in front of us the full force of the Atlantic wind. We are leaning into it to stand upright. Our windcheater hoods are flapping, our black hair streaking across our faces, salty and wet. We are shouting to each other and laughing, but our words are drowned by the crashing of the breakers over the rocks and the roar of the wind.

When I was a child growing up in Belfast we often spent the summer holidays in Donegal. Usually we stayed in a traditional cottage that was rented long-term by some friends of my parents. It was in a small village of six houses, all thatched roofed except ours, which was slated, all clustered round the communal hand-pump, where in the mornings groups of women chatted as they filled their buckets and jerry cans. There was no running water or electricity in the village. For lighting we used paraffin lamps and candles. My mother cooked on a butane stove in the corner of the living room. There was no bathroom; we washed in basins filled from buckets, and there was a chemical toilet in the stone byre opposite the house, where the turf was stored, and various tools and sacks and cans of sheep dip and paint, which must have belonged to the owner.

Like most traditional Irish cottages this one had three rooms. The middle one was the living room with its stable door to the outside and its fireplace at one end with the old and blackened cast iron potato-pot suspended on a chain above it, and the turf basket, and the shelf above with its pebbles and shells and pieces of driftwood that our friends had collected on the beach. Behind the hearth, where it was warmed by the fire, was a bedroom where my sister and I slept on two divans. Our parents' room was through a low door at the opposite end of the living room.

I remember days and days of rain; low cloud, drizzle, downpours that lasted all through one day and into the next. My sister and I put on windcheaters and took carrots and potatoes to the grey pony in the field behind the house, feeling her soft muzzle brushing our palms and breathing her damp pony smell. We played with the sheepdog puppy, Shep, and took her for walks on a length of string. And whatever the weather we went down to the beach: gathering shells, playing in the sand dunes, and (if our mother was there) swimming. Sometimes, after a swim, we'd run all the way home in our towels and stand shivering by the fire as our mother made us hot chocolate or tomato soup out of a tin.

My father usually walked, all day. In the morning he made himself sandwiches (cheese and pickle, ham), which he packed in his knapsack with a flask of tea and a map, and set out in his walking boots and anorak, striding over the hills. He walked for miles, sometimes along the cliffs to a place I'd only been to by car, a deserted fishing village at the end of a long un-tarred track: three stone houses, ruins, a rocky harbour lashed by the waves. No one lived there now, but there were some fishing boats upturned at the top of the pier and you could see the coloured floats of lobster pots bobbing about in the waves. I imagined the life they must have lived there, the loneliness, the danger when the boats put out to sea, and still now, as an adult, I picture my father sitting on the sheep-cropped grass on the cliff eating his sandwiches, silent, inconsequential amidst the shrieks of the seabirds, and the wind and the interminable breakers pounding the shore.

Twice a week in the afternoon we drove to the local market town, about ten miles away, where my mother made the long-distance call to my grandmother. Often she was gone for an hour or more, waiting in the call box for the operator to make the connection, reassuring herself that her mother, who lived on her own, was well. The three of us usually did some shopping while she was

gone and then waited in the hotel bar, my father drinking
Guinness, the two of us ginger beer. The sun would be
setting as we drove back – strips of orange and blue
amidst the blackening clouds – alongside the estuary, past
the field with the hobbled donkey, its un-pared hooves
grown to almost a foot long.

Other evenings we sat by the fire, everybody reading
except me, doing nothing, or as I now like to believe,
thinking; or playing with Shep the puppy. The evenings I
liked best were the ones when Tommy the weaver came to
visit; although I was too shy to say more than a few words
to him, I loved listening to his voice, the soft accent,
which I barely understood, and watching his bright eyes
shine in the firelight as he sipped the whiskey my father
had poured him and told us stories: about shipwrecks
whose cargo was washed up on the shore; and salmon
poaching – how they netted the estuary from boats at
night and then hauled in the nets before it got light so as
not to be seen by the Gardai. Long after my mother and
sister and I had gone to bed, I could still hear their voices,
the sound of whiskey being poured, the clink of glasses
being put down on stone.

After two weeks we packed up the car – boxes of food;
swimsuits and towels still wet and gritty with sand; trousers and jumpers acrid with turf smoke – said goodbye
to the pony and dog, and set out for home. I remember
one evening travelling through rain-slick country roads,

staring out at the looming shadows of trees, falling asleep to the flip-flop of the windscreen wipers. Then suddenly the car stopped. My father was opening his window to talk to a man in uniform who was shining his torch into the car, looking at each of us. This was the border: Nissan huts, sandbags, coils of barbed wire, a red-and-white barrier across the road with a sign that said 'STOP Customs' – and all around, searchlights.

I was scared. These were the years of the IRA border campaign. Customs posts were set alight, army barracks bombed, roads cratered, police stations riddled with bullets. In my mind I saw IRA men training with guns on rain-soaked moorlands, ambushing cars, manufacturing bombs in isolated farmhouses. Where did I get these images that plagued me at night? In those days we had no television. Had I watched the news at a friend's house or was it something my parents had said?

My father was born in Southampton to Irish parents who had come to England looking for work. His father was from a farming family near Clonakilty in County Cork. They were smallholders, 20 acres perhaps, and unusually for southern Ireland, they were Protestants. When I asked my father about this he said that perhaps they were Huguenots who had fled religious persecution in France in the eighteenth century; or they may have converted to Protestantism during the Famine in exchange for food. Whatever their origins, he said, and whatever had happened in the past, they now seemed integrated into the community, the only visible difference between them and their Catholic neighbours being that on Sundays they went to the Protestant chapel while their neighbours went to Mass.

My father rarely talked about his past but we all knew the story of how when he was seventeen he contracted tuberculosis and spent a year in a sanatorium working his way through a trunk-load of books that he kept under his bed. It was on the strength of this, he said, that he earned his scholarship to the London School of Economics – which changed the course of his life. I wish now I'd asked him more about this time. TB, in those days before antibiotics, was a life-threatening illness, yet I never once heard him mention pain, fever, blood-soaked handkerchiefs, endless nights of coughing; and surely sanatoria – even in their latter days when TB had become a cause célèbre for philanthropists and charities – were for the rich. Secretly, I think, my father, with his intellectual and socialist leanings, was delighted with the image TB conferred on him, aligning him with artists – Keats, Chekhov, the Brontë sisters, Kafka – all dead in their prime; and with the poor and underprivileged everywhere, but especially in Ireland, where generations of men, women and children – oppressed, impoverished and living in damp, over-crowded conditions – died of it.

At LSE my father specialised in Irish economic and social history. Afterwards he published his doctoral thesis *The Population of Ireland* and lectured at universities in London, Aberystwyth and Oxford (where my sister and I were born), before moving to Belfast in 1952, when I was three months old. He stayed at Queen's University (becoming Professor of Economic and Social History and publishing *Irish Peasant Society*) until his death in 1973.

When I was eight years old we went to visit my father's uncle Frank who had inherited the family farm near Clonakilty. We had been staying nearby, in Kenmare, so we set out in the morning to arrive mid-afternoon, as expected, for tea. The sun was shining weakly as we drove on winding roads that occasionally dipped down to the sea: Glengarriff, Bantry, Skibbereen, Ros Carbery. When we eventually turned off down a stony track marked by a stunted beech tree, Frank and his sheepdog came out to meet us. Unlike my father who was six foot five and thin, he was a stocky man, but he had the same blue eyes, black hair and kind questioning face. He greeted us warmly, shaking hands with my parents and pinching me lightly on the cheek: 'Hello'.

Inside the house, my great aunt Grace kissed us as we gave her the chocolates and whiskey we'd brought; then she put on her apron and started making the tea. The kitchen felt warm and familiar with its cast iron range and

intimate smell of baking, but Frank ushered us into the
parlour, which was obviously only used for guests. We sat
on the three-piece suite – my sister and I crippled with
shyness – while Frank and my father exchanged news of
relatives and talked about the farm. In time Grace and
her daughter Heather – who was younger than me with
freckles and curls – came in with the tea. Grace must
have been up early baking soda bread and scones, which
we ate with butter and homemade blackberry jam. But
despite all the kindness and willingness to embrace each
other as family, there was an awkwardness between us,
a sense that my father, with his predominantly English
accent and education, had grown too far from his roots.

After we'd finished our tea Frank said to my sister and
me, 'Would you like a ride on the pony?' Excited now,
we put on our raincoats and went outside. We found the
pony in a craggy field behind the house and Frank put
on the bridle. I remember him leading us in turns on
the stocky bay pony – with blinkers on her bridle and
no saddle because she was only used for pulling a cart
– amongst gorse bushes and outcrops of rock, with my
father and Heather walking beside us and the sheepdog
running along behind.

On the way home my father drove in silence while
my sister and I chatted excitedly about our new relatives and the windswept rocky farm. Then, when we
too were silent, my mother told us about the first time

she had met Frank and Grace. It was soon after she and my father had been married, and my father was keen to introduce her, his German wife, to Ireland and his Irish relatives. My mother had so much wanted to fit in, but Frank and Grace, in their eagerness to welcome her, had put a commode in my parents' bedroom so my mother wouldn't have to use the outside toilet like everyone else. My mother was mortified.

In Belfast we lived in a detached house with a garden, close enough to the university for my father to cycle to work. It was a middle class area, where in theory Protestants and Catholics mixed, but in practice, due to generations of discrimination in employment and education, it was, as far as indigenous Belfast residents were concerned, overwhelmingly non-Catholic. And although both my parents were non-believers and would ideally have liked us to go to a school where Protestants and Catholics mixed, in those days and still until recently, such schools didn't exist. We went instead to a school where, as far as I know (although I didn't think about these things at the time) there were no Catholic pupils. We did however have a Catholic history teacher, and I like to think that, in this overwhelmingly Unionist environment, she taught us Irish history with a compensatory nationalist slant. Certainly, in my romantic vision of Ireland, the initiators of the Easter Rising, who raised the Irish flag and proclaimed an Irish Republic in Dublin in 1916, were heroes rather than villains.

My father loved our garden and all through his life worked long hours in it. As well as the usual flower beds and lawn, he had a vegetable patch, three rows of raspberry canes, and a small apple orchard from which he made his own cider, fermenting the bruised and battered windfalls in half-barrels outside the back door, until my mother developed a stomach complaint which the doctor said was probably due to the cider. Every year at the end of May he got up early to pick great bunches of flowers – peonies, roses, delphiniums – which my sister and I proudly carried to school for the Open Day, and in September, he prepared us each a box of fruit and vegetables for the Harvest Festival. My sister and I loved the garden too, playing horses and building jumps out of bamboo canes. (A school-friend of mine still falls about laughing every time she remembers how we kidnapped the neighbourhood dogs and taught them too to show-jump.)

Of all the books our parents read to us at night it was the Irish fairy stories we loved the most; but to work properly they had to be read by our father, whose love of Ireland and its literature was palpable in the lilt of his voice and the soft Irish r's. Sitting on the edge of the bed, with my sister and I curled up together so we could both be close to him, he read about Finn MacCool, great leader of the Fianna warriors; and the Children of Lir, whose stepmother, out of jealousy, turned them into swans for 900 years. Their father never saw them again in their human form, but for the first 300 years he visited them every day as swans on the lake near his castle to tell them of his love for them.

Our house came to life at the end of May when the university term was over and the external examiners arrived to stay for the night. My mother always prepared an elaborate dinner with candles and wine and a wild Irish salmon with new potatoes and salad from the garden, and raspberry pavlova for pudding. My sister and I, when we were too young to join them, met the guests briefly and then disappeared. All through the night, as we played in the adjacent room, or woke in the small hours to go to the toilet, we could still hear their voices – the stories, the discussions, the laughter – animated by brandy and wine.

But most of the time life in Belfast was dull: grey hills, grey buildings, interminable rain and in the streets around us Protestant churches and meeting houses with repressive, god-fearing hoardings: Jesus Saves, Evil will Out, Prepare to meet thy God. Sundays were the worst: in the mornings my sister and I used to sit at our bedroom window watching people filing into the Methodist church opposite, all dressed up. After that there was nothing: shops, cinemas, pubs – any form of distraction or entertainment: closed. It has left both my sister and me with what we now call 'that Sunday feeling' – a sense of boredom, restlessness, sadness that the weekend is over and our homework still to be done. Sometimes – usually when everyone else was in the living room reading – I'd sit on the floor by the landing window, staring out over the city to Black Mountain and the Ireland beyond, dreaming.

I must have been about five and my sister seven when we went for the first time to the Twelfth of July procession, which passed the end of our street on its route from the city centre to Finaghy, on the outskirts of Belfast. Filled with anticipation, we made our way past the big house with the mad old lady who, it was said, had millions of pounds hidden in her attic until the rats ate the lot, and who frightened me each time I saw her in her long black dress and straggling hair. When we reached the main road the procession was well underway with onlookers five or six deep, some in the front row sitting on deck chairs and portable stools, with picnic baskets open beside them. Everywhere there was red-white-and-blue – people wearing it, kerb stones painted in it, Union Jacks streaming from flagpoles and upstairs windows, and high above, criss-crossing the street, strings of patriotic bunting swaying gently in the breeze.

My sister and I found a gap in the crowd and made our way to the front. Men with closed, resolute faces filed past wearing black suits, bowler hats and, of course, the archetypical orange sash. Some looked sinister with their dark glasses, white gloves and ceremonial swords, marching in silence until one or other broke the solemnity by waving and shouting to a member of the crowd. Interspersed amongst them came the marching bands playing patriotic tunes while girls and women in the crowd danced alongside, waving Union Jacks. Then, on poles high above the marchers' heads, the banners, brightly coloured silk, depicting events from loyalist history: the Siege of Derry, the Battle of the Somme, and favourite of all, King William of Orange, splashing trium-phantly across the River Boyne on his white horse having just defeated Catholic King James II, securing Protestant rule for England, Ireland and Scotland.

As far as I remember we didn't stay long, but at home all through the afternoon we could hear the drone of the crowd and the music, and still in the evening when the procession had passed, our heads rang to the tunes of 'The Sash' and 'It's a Long Way to Tipperary.' Often, in the evening, there were reports on the radio of violence – drunken, sectarian – as the marchers passed through Catholic areas, high on a victory three hundred years ago.

Sometimes, looking back on this now, I'm surprised my father allowed us to go. I never asked him about it, but I always assumed he was a nationalist and a republican, and believed that the Orange Order, with its exclusively

Protestant membership and expulsion of anyone who attended a Catholic baptism or funeral, was sectarian and its marches antagonistic. I do know, however, that he supported the Civil Rights Movement, which in the mid-sixties pointed out to the world the institutionalised sectarianism in Northern Irish society and the corruption of the Unionist government, which by redrawing electoral boundaries to marginalize the Catholic vote, had ruled unchallenged for nearly forty years. And when a group of students from Queen's University formed the People's Democracy he joined them on some of their demonstrations and sit-ins demanding equal rights for Catholics and an end to Gerrymandering.

Luckily, he wasn't with them on their Long March from Belfast to Derry, when they were ambushed by loyalists and almost a hundred people were injured. I remember listening to the news, horrified, as we learned that when the march entered Derry the violence spread, continuing all through the night until, in the morning, the police rampaged through Catholic Bogside wrecking houses and attacking people indiscriminately.

Soon afterwards, in the summer of 1969, Belfast exploded into violence. Barricades were built out of burned-out hijacked cars, old sofas, corrugated iron; explosions and gunfire echoed through the city; houses were burned down and whole areas evacuated; soldiers in armoured cars and on foot patrolled the streets while children, too young to understand, hurled stones and abuse at them. Everywhere there was suspicion, anger, hostility, and a seething sense, on both sides, of being wronged.

Maybe all this – the fear, the violence, the intractability of any solution – contributed to my father's illness. He had been diagnosed when he was younger first with 'endogenous depression' then 'manic depression.' For weeks he lay in bed, too exhausted and dispirited to move, not coming down for meals, barely eating at all. My sister and I, wrenched by his sadness, tried in every way we knew how to cheer him up. And he'd turn to us, his eyes pale with grief, and say, 'Ach sure child, can't you see? I can't go on'. One night when I got up to go to the toilet I found him sitting on the landing stairs, his head in his hands, weeping. Another time when I visited him in hospital, where the doctors wanted to give him electric shock treatment, he was sitting on a hard chair in the middle of an empty room, not even reading, and his sadness and sense of despair tore me apart. Everything he did or had ever done was useless, a waste of time, even his work, which was widely praised, was valueless.

Then came the manic phases when he thought he was invincible, and criticised us and picked arguments, and woke us at five in the morning playing Beethoven and Tchaikovsky at maximum volume. I remember him coming home from work one evening telling us excitedly that he'd seen an architect about building a house in County Cork where we could live a simple life – a plan, which, although it appealed to my sister and me, my mother thought ludicrous.

I was nervous, not sure what to expect when he asked me to spend a few days walking with him in the west of Ireland. I was 20 and at university in London, but I'd never spent time alone with him as an adult. He met me at Belfast airport – stooping to kiss me, his hand on my shoulder – and the following morning we set out in the car. After that my memories are little more than impressions: a pub where we drank Guinness in the evenings; a hotel where the owner made us sandwiches to have for our lunch; a boat trip through choppy sparkling water to Cape Clear, off the coast of County Cork. All day we walked: sometimes in silence, sometimes talking amicably. My father asked about my work at university, proud and encouraging, and told me stories from his own research: about the illegal distillation of poteen when taxes were raised in the eighteenth century; how it was brewed in secret places where a fire could be lit and there was water for cooling the still – in caves, woodlands, on islands at times when the sea was too rough for the police to set out from the mainland in boats...

Not long afterwards, when I was back in London, my sister turned up unexpectedly at my flat.

'Dad's dead.'

He'd taken an overdose of sleeping pills, which this time had worked.

After his death I didn't go to back to Ireland for a long time. My sister and I both settled in England and some years later our mother joined us. I have never identified with England, or felt I belonged, but the years passed and I was content until one day it occurred to me that nowhere I have ever been have I felt as vibrant and alive as I used to do on the west coast of Ireland. At first I didn't understand the implication of this – was it nostalgia for a lost childhood or the true meaning of 'homeland'? All I knew was that I had to go back there: to explore my Irish identity and to look for the spirit of my father in the wind and the rain and the storms that wash in over the sea.

In 1990 my husband Mark and I went to live in Donegal.

LANDSCAPE

'Well, there's Watties,' someone suggested. We were
sitting in the quiet of a Donegal pub on a wet early-
summer afternoon. In the course of the conversation
Mark had asked if there was a house or cottage nearby
we might be able to rent. At first it had seemed there was
nothing: just holiday chalets and bungalows, which were
expensive and characterless, being purpose-built to let to
tourists. We explained that wasn't what we were looking
for; we wanted to stay for a year, maybe two.

'Aye, there's Wattie's, right enough,' said the barman.

We sipped our drinks in silence as a group of men,
speaking softly in tones we probably weren't supposed
to overhear, discussed whether Wattie's was still fit to be
lived in and whether or not the owner would let it.

When I used to come to Donegal with my family this
was the part I had known and loved the best and from as
far back as I could remember had wanted to write about.
On this occasion Mark and I had been staying nearby for
almost two weeks, looking for a place to live. Everyone
we asked was curious to know what we'd be doing here

all that time, and when I explained that I had spent my holidays round here when I was a child and had always wanted to live here and write a book about it, some were suspicious, some interested, and one or two wryly commented, 'Well, you won't be the first.'

'She'd need a lick of tar on the roof, I'd say. And the nettles are probably growing in through the door.'

'That doesn't matter. We'd be happy to do some repairs.'

In time the conversation drifted on to other things. The rain was sweeping past the window in steady almost horizontal sheets. A group of Spanish tourists shuffled in, drenched, in walking boots and brightly-coloured waterproofs. After a few moments' discussion one of them came over to the bar, where we were sitting, and ordered three cups of tea and a pint of Guinness. The others, peeling off their dripping jackets and over-trousers, gratefully sat down.

'Bad day.'

They looked across and smiled, not sure what had been said, but glad of the communication.

Sometime later, when we were getting ready to leave, one of the men we'd been talking to said he'd come with us and show us Wattie's; it was on his way home. We had driven about a mile down the coast road when he indicated with a nod of his head, 'That's Wattie's'.

We wiped the condensation from the window and peered out into the mist. On a steep, grassy track leading into the hills we could just about make out a traditional cottage half-hidden by a sprawling fuchsia hedge. From what we could see it seemed ideal.

'Well, if you like it, you'd want to talk to the owner. Frank McGahern's the name.'

'I thought it was Wattie's cottage.'

'Ah for goodness' sake. Wattie's the shoemaker who lived there. He's been dead over fifty years.'

The following morning we knocked on Frank McGahern's door. When we enquired about the cottage he was friendly and invited us into his living room, but neither he nor his wife seemed keen to let it. We told them it was mainly for me, that Mark would be working in England and joining me only occasionally (which was his original plan). But that made matters worse: Wattie's wasn't fit to be lived in and certainly not by a woman alone. We tried to explain that unless it was actually falling down we'd be happy to do some repairs. But nothing changed. We had resigned ourselves to losing it when Frank's face suddenly brightened. 'If you want we'll go up there now. You can see what you think for yourselves'.

We left his house together, walked down the road a short distance, and turned up the track to Wattie's. The previous day's rain had stopped at nightfall, but the grass on the track, cropped close by sheep, was wet and slippery. Frank told us the arthritis in his knee was giving him trouble so we climbed slowly, accommodating his pace. The key to the house was kept in a stone outbuilding. Frank unlocked the door and beckoned us inside. Light filtered weakly through a clear panel on the roof. One side of the shed was piled high with tools and assorted possessions, unused, but too good to be thrown out: on the other side was a heavy wooden weaving loom. Frank told us that this was where he used to work before the new shed was built down by the house. The floor was strewn with balls of wool and bobbins and segments of rug, half-woven, then for some reason discarded. On a hook on the wall were an old school satchel and a raincoat, shrouded in dust.

Frank closed the shed door behind us and led the way to the house. We passed a heap of rubbish, sodden slug-eaten clothes and rusting beer cans, stuffed beneath the hedge, and the remains of another outbuilding whose roof had collapsed into rubble amongst split refuse sacks and brambles. At first the door refused to open. Frank kicked it sharply, and pushed as he turned the key. Inside, the house was cold and smelled of mushrooms. There was rubbish everywhere, some in carrier-bags and bin-liners, some loose. Two of the windows had been broken; one was boarded up with plywood, the other lay in shards across the floor. In places there were damp-stains on the ceiling and below them puddles filled depressions in the concrete. As we wandered around, the whole house seemed to be seething: with woodlice and spiders, and for all we knew rats and mice, and mould that grew on the walls like bark, or blistered the remaining paint as it erupted out of the stone, like great festering sores.

'Ah, this place'd be no good to you now,' said Frank, pushing aside a broken chair. 'The last ones in here let it run to ruin – towards the end they were even breaking up the furniture and using it as firewood. And then they cleared off, leaving their electricity bill unpaid and six months' rent still owing.'

But to us the house was perfect: a typical three-roomed cabin, yet unlike any I had ever been in, bright, with watery sunlight pouring in at the front, and a sort of green gloom from the small window at the back. There was even a modern bathroom – a concrete extension, with a bath and a toilet that would probably have flushed if the cistern hadn't been dry – and a solid wooden bed, and cupboards in the kitchen, built simply but with care, by someone who at some time in recent years must have enjoyed the house.

Frank seemed surprised, even disconcerted, that we still wanted to live there. I suppose, after letting the house for so many years he had now resigned himself to it lying empty, quietly decaying. At first he hesitated, unsure, then, gradually, he warmed to the idea. With some pride he pointed out the central heating system: the back boiler in the open fireplace, the hot water tank bound in blankets and insulating foil on the shelf beside it, the radiators in every room.

'Must be fifteen years that's been there,' said Frank. 'It was put in by a German, an artist, and I'm telling you some money went into that.'

'Does it still work?'

'Aye, as far as I know it does.'

Briefly he explained how the system worked and then as we stood there in the kitchen he told us about Wattie: what a fine shoemaker he had been, how at times the whole place had been filled with journeymen cobblers all cutting and stitching and making their boots around the fire; and about some of the other tenants: the writer, the artist, the German who had spent whole days fishing off the rocks at the end of the track and returning in the evening with box-loads of pollack and mackerel which he salted and laid in for the winter.

'Ah, you'll be all right here,' he said, leading the way out. Put a big fire on and you'll dry it out in no time.' He closed the door and locked it, passing the key to Mark. 'And if you cut back that auld hedge, you'll have one of the finest views in the county.'

For the following three weeks we worked on the house every day. Luckily the weather improved and we opened all the windows, filling the house with sunshine and airing it with sea wind. We lit fires in each of the three fireplaces, keeping them burning day and night. We gathered the rubbish and deposited it, in one car load after another, at the local dump. We washed down the walls and ceilings, and when they were dry, painted over the mould stains, the multi-coloured daubing of the previous tenants' children, the flamboyant red, green and yellow radiators. Everything was white.

During that time Frank came to see us often. Sometimes his wife Brid came too, just to see how we were doing and to ask if there was anything we needed. One day Frank arrived when Mark was whitewashing the outside of the house with the traditional blend of lime and cement mixed to a lumpy liquid and smeared on with a paintbrush the size of a broom. Mark's face, overalls, boots and the grass around the house were caked and splattered with whitewash. Frank seemed pleased: the house could now be seen from several miles across the bay, whereas before, grey and crumbling, it had merged forlornly with the hills. Everyone would now know that Wattie's was thriving.

Another day when Mark was repairing the roof for the second time Frank and our neighbour James from the other side both appeared. The roof had been thatched for many years and rather than continually renewing it when the thatch grew thin and slack, Frank had replaced it at some point with corrugated asbestos. That was fine, he said, until two of the tenants danced on it late one night. Ever since, it had leaked. On Frank's advice Mark had borrowed James's ladder and painstakingly sealed the cracks with tar, but soon afterwards we were woken in the night by the drip, drip, drip of water on the floor.

'Over to the left a wee bit now,' said Frank. 'Can you see that gap where the two panels meet? That's where the water's getting in.'

Mark was leaning precariously against the roof with a bucket of tar in one hand and a brush in the other. Tentatively, he moved another foot to the left.

'Aye, and around the nails as well,' said James.

Each sheet of asbestos was secured with at least a dozen nails. Mark sealed the ones he could reach and shifted the ladder.

It started to rain. Frank and James shielded their eyes, still looking up.

'And if she's still leaking now,' said Frank, 'you may get some strips of sacking, soak them in tar and seal over the whole damn thing.'

Over the months Mark tried everything but the roof always leaked. In the end we resigned ourselves to buckets and basins, shifting them about as new leaks appeared and old ones miraculously healed. And at night, kept awake by the dripping, we'd stagger out of bed, cursing, and line the buckets with towels.

Gradually the house became more comfortable. Frank lent us a mattress, some kitchen chairs and a 1950s Calor gas cooker, which he had stored in his shed for a time like this. He also gave us, as a present, a green wool rug that he had woven himself, to put beside the bed, he suggested, so in the mornings when we got up the bare concrete wouldn't be cold on our feet. Some things, such as cooking equipment, sheets, a table with detachable legs, we'd brought with us from England. Other things we found amongst the rubbish in the house: a patchwork quilt tied up in a bin-liner in the loft and remarkably free of damp and mildew, and an etching by the German artist which was abstract but unmistakably inspired by the sheep carcasses that you find amongst the hills: the fleece, horns and bones, fleshless and bleached white by the sun and salt wind

At first we were reluctant to cut down the fuchsia hedge, which was in flower, but Frank insisted, and one day I waded into it with shears and a saw only to discover hours later that most of the branches could simply be snapped off with your hand. But Frank was right: the view was outstanding. Sometimes we'd sit in total dark- ness, watching the reflection of the moon on the bay, and the house lights and the occasional car headlights crawling along on the opposite hills.

The water supply to the house came from a stream that trickled down the hill behind it. Two small reservoirs had been dug about fifteen feet apart, amongst boulders and solid outcrops of limestone. Each was lined with concrete and covered with an assortment of rusty sheet metal and rotting boards weighted down with stones. The reservoirs filtered the water at the same time as they stored it, sifting out silt and debris, which sank to the bottom. After it left the second reservoir the water was taken underground and fed by gravity to a tank in the roof of the house.

Most of the time we considered ourselves privileged to be drinking and bathing in pure water, unadulterated by chemicals, and crystal-clear except after heavy rain when it turned the colour of tea. We knew of course that a sheep could easily slip and drown and lie decaying in the stream, but we consoled ourselves that if the water was seriously contaminated the freshwater shrimps which scampered around in every glassful would suddenly be still and dead.

Occasionally, however, the system failed. One day I was washing clothes in the bath when the water slowed to a trickle and finally stopped. Frank had warned us this might happen and showed us what to do if it did. So I dried my hands and made my way up the hill. The upper reservoir seemed in order, but the lower one was almost empty with nothing coming through the black plastic feed pipe. So I put the pipe to my mouth and sucked, spitting out a trickle of warmish, peat-flecked sludge. I sucked again. This time there was a sudden spurt, almost choking me, and when I spat it out, there in the grass was a bloated dark-green leech. Shocked, it sidled away, extending to a tapered four inches, then compressing again, as gradually the tank began to fill.

When Mark went back to work in England the house felt suddenly quiet, and one long, slow afternoon I decided to dig a vegetable patch. Between the fuchsia hedge and the road there was a strip of land belonging to the cottage which Frank had said I could use. Apart from farmers, most of whom grew potatoes, few people bothered with their own vegetables, finding it more convenient to simply buy them at the local shop, and when I mentioned my garden, most replied, 'Well, I hope it grows for you,' as if they somehow knew that it wouldn't. Alternatively I was warned about the sheep which wandered freely on the hills, the roads, around the houses, even on the beach, and if they so decided could demolish a garden in minutes.

Luckily the plot had been worked before, so the rocks and boulders which studded the entire valley had already been cleared. The last time it was planted, Frank told me, was by a woman and her daughter who had gathered seaweed on the beach and carried it back in rucksacks to use as fertiliser. Now, the grass, though short, was thick and wiry, and patches of nettles spurned by the sheep were luxuriantly waist high. But the biggest problem was rushes whose entangled matted roots were as tough as leather.

In a week the blisters on my hands had hardened into painless calluses and the vegetable patch, though lumpy and uneven, was more brown than green. Sometimes when I was digging, raking, interminably sifting out roots, Frank would stand watching and tell me I was making extra work for myself; there was an easier way. But it wasn't until much later that I understood what he had meant by 'coping': you simply upturned the sods, planted the potatoes on top, and left the greenery rotting underneath as in-built fertiliser.

When the time came to fence in the vegetable patch, I suddenly noticed that the new roll of sheep wire I'd bought had disappeared. It had been lying on the grass along with a bundle of pine fencing posts close to where I was digging.

'Ah, there's blaggards in the glen as well,' said Frank when I told him about it. He sounded more upset than I was, 'They'd be better robbing a bank than taking the tools of another person's work.' And rather than letting me buy another roll he told me to ransack some of his old fences, broken down and no longer functional, around a burnt-out caravan and an old garage that someone had reversed into and partially demolished.

The fence was so difficult to put up it almost defeated me. First of all the posts had to be hammered in *outside* the vegetable patch, as the sheep would undoubtedly stretch out their necks and reach inside, and the undug ground was virtually impenetrable. Then the assorted sections of fencing that Frank let me use had to be straightened, repaired with pliers and where necessary wire coat hangers, stretched taut between the posts and finally nailed in place.

It was late evening by the time I had finished. Frank came up to see how I was doing. For a few minutes he walked around the fence, leaning against one or two of the posts to see if they wobbled, checking the tautness of the wire. Everything seemed fine and he was just explaining how to weigh down the bottom of the fence with stones, so the sheep couldn't barge underneath, when suddenly he started: 'You've put it upside down.'

I hadn't noticed that the mesh was narrower at the bottom of the fence than the top, to keep out the lambs.

'All you need now,' said Frank several days later when I was covering over the last row of Pentland Hawks, 'is your own bog.'

He was joking I think but I was immediately taken with the idea of cutting and burning our own turf.

'A fiver a month bog trespass and you can cut as much as you like for the rest of the summer.'

Bog trespass was rent paid for the use of another person's bog. Traditionally most families owned their own, but as the generations passed and land was divided, some inevitably lost out. These and newcomers to the area could apply to the council to 'open' a bog on the vast tracts of uncut bogland that covered the hills; or they could rent or more often borrow a bog. Some people simply took matters into their own hands and started working one of the many bogs that emigrants had abandoned but not yet relinquished in case one day they or their children chose to return.

'I don't suppose there'd be an unused bog we'd be able to rent.'

'Ah for heaven's sake I was pulling your leg. There's the bog that Wattie once worked. If you want it it's yours for the cutting. I'm too old to go up there with you now, but if you ask him maybe Conor would show you what to do.'

Conor, another neighbour who later became a close friend, agreed and the following evening Frank took the two of us down to the shed by his house and gave us a turf spade or *sleán,* a plastic fish box about the size of a laundry basket, two wooden sticks to use as markers, and an improvised 'line' made of a dozen or so strands of different coloured wool. Then he explained to Conor exactly where the bog was and the two of us set off in the car. We drove about half a mile down the coast road, then walked up a gentle slope that led to the hills.

The bog was easy to find. It was ragged and overgrown and obviously hadn't been cut for years, and apart from one equally long-abandoned bog nearby, was on its own. Conor, using his wellingtons, measured two and a half feet back from the cut face at either end of the bog, marked the points with sticks and attached the line between them. Then with a sharpened garden spade he cut right round the three sides of the marked rectangle and began to strip the top layer from the bog, 'paring' it.

'That's called the *scra*,' he shouted, throwing back great clumps of grass, heather, rushes and their peat-embedded roots. 'You can dry it and burn it, but it's poor quality turf. All right, I suppose, for damping down the fire at night.'

Conor was working fast and in less than an hour the two of us were standing on the newly exposed seam of turf. It was smooth and level and as softly resilient as a mattress.

'Now boy,' said Conor, rubbing his hands together, 'where's that turf spade?'

He picked up the *sleán* and cut seven or eight perfect rectangles of turf, throwing them straight off the spade onto the bank behind him, where they landed, unbroken, in a tidy heap.

Then it was my turn. There was no comparison with digging a garden; the *sleán* consisted of two narrow blades at right angles to each other on a wooden shaft, and you didn't have to force it into the ground or use your foot, you simply sliced the turf like chocolate cake. It was difficult at first to cut the pieces the same size so the rows stayed even, and more often than not they broke or slipped down from the *sleán* as I threw them behind me. But it wasn't strenuous.

Conor watched as I cut several more rows, working slowly in from the open face towards the bank. Then he fetched the fish box: 'You're going to have to spread it on the hillside, I'm afraid.' He nodded in the direction of a steep slope. All the flatter ground around the bog was saturated. He rummaged in his pocket and found some nylon baling twine which he tied to one end of the fish box while I loaded the turf. Then we dragged the fish box up the hillside, emptied it, and spread the cut turf to dry amidst the grass and the crisp scraggy heather.

After that I went to the bog every day. Sometimes I walked over the hills behind the house, scrambling up past the two reservoirs, alongside the stream, then where the ground levelled on the brow of the hill, on a track known as the bog road, a short-cut to the next village. But usually I took the easier route on the coast road, passing the pier with its upturned boats and stacks of lobster pots, then as I climbed, gazing down from the cliffs and out over the sea.

For at least a week the sun shone every day and most people took advantage of it, cutting their turf. The main road out of the village, flanked on either side with bogs, looked like a picnic site, with parked cars and people milling around, talking and working. Suddenly everyone was sunburned, some of them painfully, not realising, they said, the strength of the sun through the cool sea wind. Children's faces, which one day were as pale as soapstone, were pink and riddled with freckles the next.

Still the work didn't seem hard, only monotonous. There were eight pieces of turf to a row. I cut twelve, one-and-a-half rows, throwing them straight up into the fish box. Then I laid down the *sleán* and carted the load uphill. Each time I followed the same route, avoiding the marshy area deeper than my boots, the grassy tussock which stopped the load in its tracks, and the diagonal shortcut so steep it upturned it. In the past they would have carried the turf in wooden wheelbarrows or in creels on their backs or on donkeys. Nowadays, although one family owned a little motorised buggy, most people used fish boxes. But as far as I know there were few bogs where the only dry ground was uphill.

Gradually I learned how to pace the work. If I carried even one or two pieces of turf too many, the fish box refused to move and by the time I had struggled up the hill and emptied it, I felt irritated and tired without really knowing why. But in time I learned to be patient, to relax into the natural rhythm of the work and stop fighting it with devised schemes to be faster, more efficient. I thought about other things, or switched off my mind so it no longer synthesised, merely absorbed: the texture of the turf, the new shoots pushing up through the straw-coloured rushes under my feet, the yellow tormentil and clumps of bog moss so pale it was almost white. Sometimes I'd sit and rest for a while with a flask of tea and some sandwiches, or I'd lie on my back on a waterproof jacket, watching the larks singing high in the sky and seagulls casting shadows under the sun.

The heat was followed by three or four days' rain. Afterwards the turf was soft and loose and easy to cut, but the bog itself was a mess. At one end water was trickling down in a steady stream on to the cut face where I was working. When the weather was dry I hadn't noticed the drainage ditch which channelled water from the marshy ground above straight down over the bog. Nor had I seen that, in the corner, where over the years the water had accumulated, there was a pool with frogspawn, and bog pondweed, and a greasy surface-film from the oil in the turf.

For a bog to develop there has to be wetness: rain, and on the coast the added moisture blown in from the sea. Dead plants, because they are constantly waterlogged, only partially decompose, so forming peat. The rain, over the years, washes nutrients down through the soil, leaving the surface acid and virtually sterile. Few plants thrive: sphagnum moss, purple moor grass, heather, black bog rush, sedge – all of them acid-loving, all deriving minerals from outside the soil, from the wind and rain, or like the sundew and butterwort, from insects which they trap and ingest.

Some bogs are ten or twelve spades deep: so deep that a man cutting the bottom layer would have to be twice his own height to look out over the top. Our bog was four spades' deep. The turf at the bottom was almost black and so smooth and soft you could pick it up and shape it with your hands, or squeeze it so it oozed between your fingers. But half of it was underwater and as I slopped about in the muck, scooping spadefuls of dripping sludge off the rock, I suddenly felt ridiculous. Maybe the previous layer ought to have been the last; but this was the best turf, drying like brick and burning slowly, almost smokelessly, with as much heat as coal.

So I persevered, each time dragging only seven or eight pieces of this heavier turf up the now slippery track, smearing my hands and clothes and even my face with black grease, like engine oil.

Because in a bog dead plants never fully decay, each layer – in the pollen, leaves, seeds it contains – describes its own history. Bogs developed because of the climate, but cultivation helped them to spread. Five thousand years ago there were forests which dried out the soil, but itinerant farmers ring-barked the trees, so the canopy died, bringing light to their crops. When rain – and the crops – had depleted the soil, the farmers moved on. More land was exposed. Iron, washed down through the soil by the rain, formed a residue neither roots nor water could penetrate. And although some of the trees grew back in the wake of the farmers, the forests, their roots flooded with water, gradually died.

And as the bogs spread, grew deeper, they encapsulated

more of the past: court tombs, the burial chambers of the first stone age farmers; portal tombs, those of their successors a thousand years later; Celtic ring forts and stone barrows and the monastic settlements of early Christians who were ascetics spending long periods in solitary contemplation and were drawn to the west of Ireland by the rugged beauty of the countryside. Some of the burial chambers were discovered by people simply walking in the hills, who trod on a flat stone – the roof – half buried and hidden in the heather.

And as I was digging I thought about other things people had found: stone axe-heads, pottery, flint arrowheads, Celtic gold- and silverwork, butter buried in wooden casks or in bark or cloth – no one knew why; corpses maybe thousands of years old, but with clothes, skin, nails preserved as if they'd been recently buried.

Several days of sun and wind followed and I turned the cut turf, letting the underside dry. It was harder work than cutting and spreading – continually bending to pick up each piece, one at a time, turning it over, setting it down so no two pieces touched. When the 'good drying' continued and a skin had formed on both sides of the turf, I built it into clusters called 'footings' – six or seven pieces arranged vertically so they leaned in at the centre in the shape of a wigwam for the wind to blow through and ventilate.

The last of the trees had been felled over three hundred years ago. Now the hills were as bare as sand dunes, although whole forests had been buried in the bogs. Until recently people excavated building timber, recognising a fallen tree by the lack of dew on the grass above, assessing its length and width with a probe, digging away the surrounding turf and hauling the tree out with rope. The wood, although thousands of years old, was as hard as stone. Some of the older houses were still roofed with bog timber. Furniture was made of it, milk churns, gates, even boats.

When I had finished building the footings I started to pare another section of bog. It had seemed easy when Conor was doing it, as though the foot or so of *scra* on top was a different consistency from the turf beneath and could be stripped away like peel from an orange. But with me, this didn't happen; each clod, although I had sliced around it first, was bound down with roots and the only way to remove it was to carve into the turf beneath, wasting it, and leaving the top layer hacked up and uneven. I was glad our bog was on its own, that no-one was watching. People prided themselves on tidy bogs; ours was like a bomb-site.

In the past people used a layer of *scra* as roofing insulation between timber and thatch. Even now, although Wattie's was no longer thatched, most of the *scra* was still in place and occasionally I'd be woken in the middle of the night by a loud thump on the roof. The first time I heard it I was terrified, thinking it was either an intruder or the roof caving in, but Conor assured me it was only the *scra,* which soaked up moisture and expanded when the weather was wet, and then when it was dry shrank again, tumbling into the roof cavity.

Gradually the summer wore on. Orchids appeared and asphodel and tufts of white cotton-grass dotted over the hills. I didn't cut turf every day: sometimes it was too wet and afterwards midges clung to the bogs like heat-haze. Then it was too windy, or so still that black flies and clegs followed me around, biting and pestering. Other days I went to the bog intending to work but after twenty minutes gave up, exhausted or simply not in the mood.

In July Mark came back, this time for good. I had enjoyed working the bog on my own, spending whole days lost in contemplation, but it was good too to have company, and it was faster with two people: one cutting, the other spreading. People said that two strong men working like this could save a year's turf in a couple of days, but most people took it more easily, working now and again throughout the summer. Some cut more turf than they needed in case they were ill or the weather was bad the following year. Others hired machinery: tractors, which raked out the turf and in hours laid it in tracks over acres of hillside. The tracks broke down as they dried into cylindrical sections known as 'sausages'. But these still had to be turned and footed and stacked, and although the machines didn't visibly damage the surface, no-one really knew what, year after year, they'd do to the bogs.

'Have you your turf won yet?' people started to ask in August.

Already tractors were trundling down from the bogs, their overloaded trailers spilling turf as they bounced over the potholes. But we were still cutting.

'You'd want to get a move on so. There'll be rain on the way by the end of the month.'

Glancing over the hillside, calculating, we knew that our flimsy heaps of turf, dried and shrunken now, and hidden amongst the heather, would all be burned in a matter of months. We doubled our efforts. Elsewhere people were traipsing back and forth across the bogs building small heaps and footings into one big 'lump' by the road, ready to be shovelled into the trailer. At home, those who didn't have sheds were arranging the turf in stacks, one piece at a time, with the help of a ladder. Some of the stacks were so carefully constructed, the pieces so regular, they were water-resistant. Others were draped over with fishing nets or tarpaulins, weighted down with old car tyres and stones.

All through September it rained. Then, in October, after the first dry period of four or five consecutive days, we gathered the turf into two piles. The piles were bigger than we had anticipated but the turf, especially the dark rich bottom layer, was so brittle now it was dry that it broke apart when we loaded it into the fish box and again as we emptied it onto the pile.

'Aye, with that kind of turf,' said Frank, when we asked his advice, 'you'd need to bag it – unless you want to be burning peanuts all through the winter.'

So we borrowed as many fertiliser bags as we could and spent most of the following day filling them and stacking them carefully with the edges turned in to keep out the rain. For the rest of the month the bog was so wet that the tractor – or the heavy trailer behind it – would have got stuck. We waited. We tidied the byre in readiness.

When the day came – cold, clear, almost frosty – I didn't go to the bog. I could carry a bag of turf a short distance but I couldn't have lifted it on to the trailer. Conor had kindly offered to help and when the tractor, driven by another neighbour, Eamon, pulled up on the road, he and Mark set off down the track and clambered aboard.

Several hours later the tractor laboured up the hill, turned and drew to a halt. Eamon climbed out and Conor jumped from the trailer ready to receive the bags as Mark passed them down. Then, before they went back for another load, we carried the bags to the shed and emptied them. It was a slow process: one heavy bag at a time. With breaks for rests and cups of tea and sandwiches we worked until it was almost dark and the cold was setting in.

The turf burned well. On frosty mornings if we built a fire of the darkest, best quality turf, in less than an hour the back boiler would thump and churn, and if we switched on the electric pump, silencing it, hot water would flood through the pipes, gurgling and clicking, to every radiator in the house. In time we learned how to keep the fire burning overnight: we simply blanketed the embers with a thick layer of ash when we went to bed and in the morning we raked them over until they glowed again, kindling the turf that we had set around the hearth to warm and dry.

In autumn the bog grasses turned red. On clear days, in the last of the evening sunlight, the hills were the colour of amber. Then for weeks there was rain, slow interminable drizzle and cloud so low that you felt you were drowning. Even the occasional downpours, sudden and violent, seemed a relief. The mist was eventually broken by cold north-easterly gales bringing hail and sleet and a short-lived coating of snow. In January a flock of wild swans settled on one of the clear bog lakes where in summer we fished for trout.

GATHERING CARRAGEEN

I met Margaret in May. She was standing by the road about five miles from where I lived and as the car approached she very tentatively lifted just the fingers of one of her hands. It was the way that many older people asked for a lift, being too proud or modest to stick out their thumbs and entreat you with eye-contact in the common language of hitch-hikers. She'd been waiting for the bus, she said, as if to apologise, but it was late and she had to be at the dispensary before it closed at midday.

We chatted. After a while it emerged that we were both on our own at that time. Her husband had died suddenly just a few years previously and Mark was back in England. Neither of us had any children.

'Why don't you come over and see me sometimes?' she said. 'You could come any time. Or come on a Sunday – that's when it's nice to have visitors.'

She paused, sparing my concentration for a disorienting succession of double bends. Then, when the road ahead was clear, she carefully described where her house was, what it looked like, the various landmarks along the way.

Before she got out she took some coins from her purse and pressed them towards me with such insistence that my refusal had to become forceful.

'I knew that you'd come today,' she said one Sunday not long afterwards as she greeted me at the door with a kiss. 'I burned the bread last night and they say that's a sure sign a stranger will come to the house.'

As she took me inside, her Yorkshire terrier scurried about at our feet, yapping excitedly. 'That's Bruno,' she said, sitting me down by the range and opening the door to throw another lump of turf on the fire.

We sat and talked for a while. Then she put on her apron and busied herself between the kettle, set to boil on the range, and the small kitchen next door. Our conversation shrank to occasional comments exchanged between rooms as she laid the table with plates and cups, dishes of butter and jam, milk, sugar, biscuits and cake. Finally she brought in the soda bread, smiling as she held it up so I could see for myself the charred currants poking jaggedly out of its darkened crust.

Margaret herself didn't eat, she didn't even have a cup of tea, but she kept refilling my cup and encouraging me to have another biscuit or a piece of cake. When she was finally satisfied that I had finished she took the things back to the kitchen and spent a few minutes putting away food and washing dishes.

'It's full moon tomorrow,' she said as she came back. 'They'll be down at the shore gathering dillisk and carrageen.'

At first I had visions of people gathering seaweed by the light of the moon, maybe a traditional fair with dancing and singing. I had never lived by the sea before and it took me some time to understand the significance of the moon for shore-dwellers: that at each full and new moon the tides are both higher and lower than usual, and that these spring tides, as they are called, are especially marked when the gravitational pull of the sun on the sea is in direct line with that of the moon.

'Will we go – the two of us?'

'I'd love to.'

'Ring me tomorrow. I'll find out the best place to go and the times of the local tides.'

'Is that my friend?' said her voice on the phone the following morning, then louder, more urgently, 'Can you come over soon? The tide is almost out.'

When I arrived she was waiting. It looked as though she had been up and busy for several hours and had finished all her household chores: the living room was poised in perfect order between meals, between all activities. She put on her coat and a pair of walking shoes, found some plastic bags in a drawer in the kitchen, and on the way out blessed herself with holy water from a small container in the porch.

We were in good spirits as we drove down to the sea. The sun was edging further out from the clouds than it had in days, and the colours of the countryside, bathed in both sunlight and water, were startlingly bright. We left the car and walked across a stretch of rocky grassland dotted with campion and clumps of thrift. Soon we could feel the sea wind in our faces and moments later we were looking down over a tiered ledge of rock that stretched right out into the bay. A mass of seaweed on the lower tier framed the shore with a rippling brown fringe.

'Be careful,' said Margaret, who was slightly ahead of me. We were ankle-deep in swathes of tangle weed. It was harder to keep our footing than it would have been walking on ice, and in places the growth was so dense that it masked fissures and rock pools so we had to test the ground gingerly before taking each step. Mountains of spaghetti-like bootlace weed and the long flat fronds of *laminaria saccharina*, which looked like giant sheets of freshly boiled lasagne, made it suddenly seem as though we had walked into an Italian chef's anxiety dream.

'Do you know what it looks like?' Margaret asked me.

I didn't. So she delved under armloads of weed and picked a dark curly tuft. 'That's carrageen,' she said, as she held it out for me. Then, a few yards ahead, she pulled some purplish ribbons off the rock. 'And that's dillisk.' She bit into a piece and passed me another. It was the texture of a thin sliver of rubber and tasted of salt and fish and the smell of the sea.

Now that I knew what I was looking for we were able to wander off on our own, each filling our bags. Margaret had said it was still a bit early for dillisk and carrageen – there'd be more of it in August – but having to search was part of the pleasure. Even out of the water everything was wet and shiny as though it was coated with glycerin: the weed, the red and orange sea-anemones that clung to the rocks amongst it, the outcrops of mushroom-like holdfasts from which strands of thong-weed had either broken off or not yet sprouted.

I was gazing into a rock pool watching a shoal of semi-transparent fish darting in and out of the shadows when suddenly I noticed a clump of carrageen with blue phosphorescence on its fronds. I picked it and the colour vanished, then dropped it back into the water and watched the bright blue reappear as slowly it sank to the bottom.

Straightening up, I made my way to the water's edge.

'Don't fall in,' called Margaret, seeing me there. I had never asked how old she was; she could have been in her seventies, but on those treacherous rocks she was as sure-footed as a girl.

My bags were almost full and slowly I wandered over to join her.

When we were back in the car she surprised me by saying, 'Will we go to the Blue Lagoon for dinner now?'

The Blue Lagoon was a bar and a nightclub and the only restaurant for miles around. As we went inside, it took a while for our eyes to adjust to the sombre lounge with its dark blue walls, red carpet and red plush seating. It was designed for the night and not the day and it was easy to imagine a band and a crowd of people on the dance floor, their white shirts and dresses radiant under ultra-violet strobes. We sat at a table by the window and ordered fish and chips. We didn't talk much as we waited, just stared contentedly out at the sea and the motionless silhouettes of distant boats.

The carrageen had to be spread outside to dry; the dillisk did too, but the procedure was different. Carrageen was left for several days, day and night, in the rain and dew as well as the sun, but dillisk had to come in at night and could be ruined if the weather wasn't fine enough to more or less dry it the day after it had been picked. The reason for the difference was that dried dillisk should still taste of salt and fish, whereas carrageen ought to be bland, the flavours of the sea washed away with the rain.

The dillisk dried. The carrageen had to be turned every morning and after every shower. Gradually the colour drained from it, brown becoming white tinged with the watery flush of pink, orange and green. There were times when I almost despaired, seeing it sodden and hissing with flies and then one morning after a night of rain I found it speckled with mould. But just in time the sun came out and by the end of that day it was crisp and dry with only a few rotten patches that were easy to pick out and throw away.

Margaret said that she had a carrageen drink every night before she went to bed: it was nutritious and good for colds and flu. To make it, she explained, you mix half-water, half-milk in a pan, add a pinch of dried carrageen and boil it for three or four minutes until it thickens. Then you strain it into a cup and add sugar. If you vary the proportions and leave it to set in a bowl overnight you can make Irish moss, or carrageen moss, a kind of blancmange.

Dillisk was usually chewed dry. One old man told me that he always took a pocketful with him when he went to the pub 'to complement the beer'.

The fishing season was heralded by gannets soaring majestically over the bay, higher than any other seabird. Every so often one would fold its wings round its body as tightly as leaves wrap a corn cob and plummet into the sea. Moments later it would surface, gulp down a fish and take off, its heavy wing-beats slapping the waves.

Mackerel and pollack approached the shore as soon as the land had warmed, in May. Coalfish or *glasán* came later, towards the end of summer. By November all had disappeared, seeking the warmth of deeper waters and their breeding grounds in the open sea.

Right around the coast, almost every rock, point, inlet and cliff had its name. The best rod-fishing spots were Leic na Magach, Ramatia, the Gub, the Tearáil, and from one day to the next, fishermen weighed up the relative merits of each according to the time of day, the tide, the direction of the wind, the strength of the ground swell. At the pub in the evening they would often compare their success:

'Were you down the day?'

'Aye, I was three hours at Ramatia. Nothing. One tiddler which I fed to the cat.'

'They say Paddy Joe killed seven down the Gub.'

'The water was dirty enough.'

'Aye, and a strong sou'west in it too.'

And so the fund of experience amassed by generations gradually evolved with the changing conditions at sea. Tackle was changing as well: most younger people used modern fibreglass rods, with reels and nylon line and either rubber sand eels or reflective metal lures. Older men, typically shunning the shops and unnecessary expense, often made do with a bamboo pole, a length of cod-line and a fly of unspun wool, with maybe a strand or two of red thread running through it. Without a reel, they simply laid down the rod when they caught a fish and pulled in the line, hand over hand. In a sense theirs was the connoisseur's method; with no casting or trawling they were free to sit in the sun, smoking a cigarette, as they watched the pollack glide about in the bottom-weed and waited for one to bite.

But even the most experienced fishermen admitted there was more to it than tackle and knowing the right conditions: you needed luck. Many a day I'd go to the recommended place at a particular time and spend three hours or more watching the light change as the tide filled and turned and not get a single bite, while on either side of me people were reeling in one pollack after another: 'It's a question of attitude,' they sometimes told me, or alternatively, 'You have to sing to them.'

Then one evening I went to Leic na Magach against all advice. Nothing much had been caught for some time and it was assumed there were simply no fish around. But it had been an oppressively hot day and whether I caught anything or not, the cool breeze and the open view of the sea were pleasant and soothing.

The first time I cast I caught the connecting rope between a lobster pot and its buoy. I pulled and yanked but couldn't free the hook and in the end I had to cut through the line, abandoning my lure and tying on a new one. The second time I felt a bite. Then the line started to slew from left to right as I reeled it in; sometimes there was pressure, sometimes not and for a while it was impossible to tell whether the fish had escaped or even whether the bite I had felt had been merely the pull of the waves. Then I saw a flash of silver and felt the unmistakable tug of a fish darting for shelter amidst the shadows and weed. Very carefully, knowing that unless the fish was perfectly hooked it was at this stage I would lose it, I eased it out of the water and up over the sheer face of the rock. It was a mackerel.

My excitement turned to horror as I watched the fish thrashing about on the rocks, its gills straining rhythmically as it suffocated out of the water. I tried to catch it to take out the hook, but the silver and green stripes twisted and slithered out of my grasp. I tried again, this time gripping the gills firmly. For an instant the body flapped convulsively, then it was still. I tugged at the hook with my other hand; it had been swallowed cleanly and by the time it was freed the fish was dead.

I cast again and caught another mackerel. It must have been at this time or soon afterwards that I realised the sea was teeming with them. If the water had been calmer I would have seen shoals of them playing, interference patterns on the surface that looked like the wind until you realised they were too localized and moved too suddenly. There were seabirds everywhere: bobbing up and down on the waves, standing watch on the rocks, gliding purposefully over the water, then suddenly swooping in clusters as they fought for a fish.

But it wasn't just mackerel. At one point I saw a shoal of what must have been *glasán* fleeting past the base of the rock. Then I felt the thrill of an unmistakable pull, the aggressive strength of a much bigger fish. As I hoisted the struggling weight from the water my rod bent precariously and my much-abused reel started to slip and then refused to engage at all, so I ended up lifting rather than winding the fish up the side of the rock. But I landed it safely. A pollack.

Again I felt the horror, recoiling from this frantically thrashing creature, yet knowing that now I had caught it I'd have to remove the hook. It was almost somersaulting now in its attempts to return to the sea. I grabbed it behind the gills, squeezing the firm flesh tightly and reached into its gaping mouth. The hook was so deeply embedded that it took a long time to extract. Afterwards the fish was still very much alive and at first I took the easy option of just turning my back, but that didn't seem right. The best fisherman I know once said if you killed a fish by bashing its head on the rocks the adrenalin that produced would ruin the flavour, but if you broke its neck and left it to bleed the meat would be clean and white. So I reached for the fish again, inserting the first two fingers of my right hand into the peony flaps of its gills and, looking in the other direction, pulled backwards. It was a big fish and I almost hadn't the strength. When it eventually died I was shaking.

A breeze blew in from the sea as I cast again and I realised it had started to drizzle. The horizon drew nearer, blurred by cloud, and for a while all I could see were the waves lurching rhythmically into the rocks then falling away with occasional splashes of white. The tide turned. My luck continued. With each fish there was the same rush of adrenalin, the excitement as it approached the shore of the first glimmer of recognition: a mackerel's white underbelly, the pure grey of a *glasán,* the very slight reddish tinge of a pollack; and then the aftermath of taking out the hook and either actively killing the fish or watching its slow suffocation.

The rain stopped and the cloud lifted. A watery sun and a few strips of orange appeared on the horizon; the beach and the village behind it were momentarily bathed in its light. I gathered up the fish and walked home over the rocks and the boggy sheep-cropped fields.

Everyone was surprised that the mackerel had come in as far as Leic na Magach. Usually if you wanted mackerel you went to the Tearáil or the Gub and fished in the open sea as opposed to the bay. They were surprised, too, at my luck; it had been a bad summer for fish. Almost everyone could remember when times had been better, when three men fishing together would easily have taken sixty or more. A few spoke nostalgically of bringing home *galachs* of fish – *ludars* the lot of them. In those days they cured the fish; filleted them, washed off all traces of blood so they wouldn't rot, and laid them flat between layers of salt until they were as dry as leather. Mackerel, when cured, turn red and a 'rusty mackerel' in winter with a plate of spuds and butter was considered 'a mighty feed altogether'. A few people still salted fish, others stored them in freezers, but really there was only one rod-fisherman now who caught more than he ate in the summer.

'It's the pair trawlers,' he explained to me. 'You see them going back and forth at the mouth of the bay. Nothing gets past them. Hundred-footers most of them and so laden with fish they can hardly float.'

'My-oh,' said Margaret when I told her about all the fish I had caught. 'You must have had some fun down there.'

'I did, but I felt a bit guilty, like a mass murderer.'

'Ah well, you shouldn't be doing it then.' She seemed quite clear about this; to me it wasn't so simple.

Margaret loved fresh fish and I had saved the biggest pollack for her. She told me that when she was first married a man used to come to the door selling sprats and he'd fill up a glass sweet jar for six pence. Nowadays she bought her fish from the fish lady who delivered once a week and whose yellow van was stocked with almost every fish she could think of. Sometimes she showed me some trout that she had bought, or a 'nice piece of ling'. Like many of the older people I knew, Margaret wasn't keen on mackerel. I assumed it was simply their flavour or oiliness until someone told me about a body that had once been washed up covered with mackerel like quivering tadpoles at a lump of meat.

'How do you cook your pollack?' I asked her as she lifted the lid off the range and moved the kettle onto the hot plate.

'I boil it, half-milk, half-water. Some people add an onion. Or else I tie it in a bag and steam it. You can salt it overnight as well and then steep it in cold water for an hour or two before you boil it.'

'It's much better for you like that. We always fry ours.'

She went into the kitchen. I could hear her rustling paper and slicing bread. Sometimes I told her not to bother with anything to eat, that I had just had breakfast or lunch and the tea by itself would be great. But it made no difference. While she was busy, I played with Bruno for a minute or two and then sat in silence, absorbing the quiet order of her living room: the sacred heart on the wall, the wooden pendulum clock that no longer worked, the patchwork cushion covers that she had made on the treadle sewing machine in the corner.

When she had brought everything through she poured me a cup of tea and sat down. We talked while I spread butter and jam on slices of bread, and ate.

During the two or three days of spring tides, Mark and I sometimes asked people where the best places were for gathering shellfish. Like seaweed, types of shellfish were unevenly distributed around the coast.

Whelks, which we sought one overcast day in September, were within walking distance. We could have followed the gentle slope of the river-bed, over the moor to the sea, but we took the short-cut, scrambling down a craggy cliff on a path that was barely discernible after years of disuse. At the bottom we joined the river on a stony beach littered with driftwood and debris that had been washed up in storms and abandoned out of reach of the tide.

Beyond the shoreline a swamp of brown weed rose and fell with the waves and a convoy of eider ducks, unaware of our presence, cruised down a clear channel through it.

There were a few whelks where we were standing at the mouth of the river, but we had been told they would be bigger and more plentiful beyond the point, so we wandered on. The rocks were olive green and ochre and so slippery that the only way to walk on them was to aim for the cement firmness of limpets and barnacles. It was three days since the full moon and the tide was no longer particularly low so as we rounded the point we had to edge our way slowly, holding on to the cliff, while the water lapped at our feet.

On the other side of the point was a second inlet, perfectly contained by cliffs. Fulmars were circling in front of the higher ledges and occasionally gliding in to land. In the shadows beneath, the air felt dank, and the light, on the already overcast day, seemed filtered through green. Somewhere water was dripping and the sound echoed hollowly over the rocks.

There were whelks everywhere. So many we could scoop them up in both of our hands, or if we'd had a shovel we could have shovelled them into our bag. On flat surfaces they were strewn like pebbles; elsewhere they clung to the rock, not tightly like limpets, but so there was a slight squelching sound as we peeled them away.

We filled our bags and then spent a few minutes searching for carrageen and dillisk amongst the weed and the anemone-studded rock pools. But we didn't stay long. The only access was the way we had come, and if the tide had turned we would have been stranded. So we made our way back, slithering over the rocks and round the point where the ledge was already inches narrower than before.

For cockles we went further, almost an hour's drive away, to the place I had often stayed as a child: six or seven houses clustered between mountains and pale windswept sand dunes. In those days the road over the mountains was un-tarred and barely passable with potholes and rushes, and the houses had no electricity or running water. We parked amongst five or six tourist cars by the side of the road, and as I opened the door and got out, the smell of turf smoke on the sea air reminded me of the clattering hand looms you used to hear in the shed behind each of the houses, and Tommy the Weaver, who sometimes came and drank whiskey with my father and talked by the fire until the early hours of the morning.

Surprisingly, not much had changed. Thatched roofs had been replaced with slates and tiles, the communal pump was now stiff with disuse, and quite a few of the houses were obviously only occupied by holiday-makers in summer. But there was still no shop or pub, and the acres of beach would probably always be excessively exposed for swimmers and sunbathers.

We set off down a sandy path along the back of the village, past the house where I used to stay with my family and the field where my sister and I fed potatoes and carrots to Misty the pony. Memories flooded back as we clambered through the soft sand into the dunes, then slithered down the other side leaving footprints like craters. When we came out at the estuary, the tide was as low as I had seen it, with only a narrow channel of water flowing sluggishly through the broad trough of sand.

We took off our shoes. The sand was cool and damp with little hard ridges left by the waves. There were cockle shells all around but most of them had been opened and emptied by the birds. So we waded up to our ankles in the warm water, and squatting down, scratched the surface of the sand until we came across a closed shell that felt like a nut. Usually there were three or four together just below the surface, before the sand gave way to a deeper layer of mud and silt. The shells were striped in the colours of the sand and the mud: from pale flaxen, that was almost white, to a dark bluish grey.

Another day, in search of mussels, we went further round the coast to a long narrow headland. We took the car as close to the point as we could and then walked along a stony track through the fields to where we understood the mussels would be. It was a bright windy day. The sea on three sides was picture-book blue with white crests chasing about with the waves. As we walked, sudden gusts of wind came tearing over the headland, buffeting us with such strength that we reeled as though we were drunk. Maybe it was the sunshine, maybe the unusual clarity of the light that made me notice so many flowers: harebells, meadowsweet and montbretia blowing about in the grass, fuchsia and honeysuckle in the hedges.

We were beginning to wonder if we had gone the wrong way when we saw a man coming towards us with a dog.

'It's a beautiful spot you've got here.'

'Aye, not so grand in winter.' I imagined the same wind, driving rain and hail, day after day.

We chatted; about the weather, about our home in England, about the years he had spent in Australia.

After a while we realised he must be wondering what we were doing here, not least on his land. 'We were looking for mussels.'

'Ah, you're away out. You want to be over in the channel.' He directed us back to the headland, pointing the way with his stick that was a length of plastic piping. 'Turn left at the school and ask at the last house there.'

We knocked at the door and a grey-haired couple, after a few minutes consideration, sent us through some boggy fields to a stream which eventually came out at the estuary, a broad expanse of mud and bladderwrack.

It's a bit glarey,' they warned us. 'You'll be all right if you keep to the weed.'

The mud was soft and loose and we sank in up to the top of our boots. We didn't want to venture out too far, so we scrambled about amongst the bladderwrack and rocks at the mouth of the stream. To get to the mussels we had to peel back curtains of khaki weed, and identical coloured crabs, suddenly exposed, sidled speedily back under cover. The mussels were caked in barnacles and grew in clusters attached to each other and the base of the rock. A nauseating smell filled the air: of warm seaweed and salt-water evaporating off the mud.

'They used to make a kind of soup out of whelks,' said Margaret one afternoon when I was visiting her. 'Or you could use limpets as well. You boiled the whelks for a few minutes, then prized them out of the shells with a needle and added butter, milk and corn flour to thicken it. *Moarach* it was called.'

Margaret said that she didn't really like shellfish and I had to agree – although I loved gathering them and tried to enjoy eating them. Mark was keen on them and those we couldn't eat we gave to friends. A lot of people didn't like cockles and mussels, although perhaps because they were local, most were fond of whelks. But with one or two exceptions no one gathered shellfish anymore.

The conversation dwindled, then died. I had finished eating, finished my second cup of tea and Margaret seemed happy, for once, to leave the plates on the table. She was sitting warming her legs by the range, with Bruno asleep at her feet. After a while I asked her what spring tides had been like when she was a child: if there were other things people had gathered on the shore. I wanted her to tell me how they used to go down to the beaches with horses and carts, collecting seaweed to fertilise the potato fields; how in winter they amassed great heaps of seaweed to sell to the agent from the local factory; how when times had been hard some of the men used to trap nesting seabirds on the cliffs and gather their eggs; how people killed seals in the underwater caves where they bred, claiming the government bounty, then hanging the carcass by the fire so the fat dripped down into a pot to be stored away and used as a rheumatism cure. I wanted her to describe to

me a way of life I had only read about, before the only real
value of the shore was in tourism.

But she didn't. She told me she knew nothing at all
about that: that although she lived so close to the sea she
was really a mountain person. And thinking back over
the time we had known each other, I realised it was true.
When I had told her about the storms I loved watching
from my window – the great waves smashing over the
rocks, the sweeping blow-back of their spray – she said
she wouldn't enjoy that. She preferred her own view: the
peaceful consistency of the hills.

PILGRIMAGE

I was nervous about going to Lough Dearg. I knew it was supposed to be the hardest Christian pilgrimage in the world and that it entailed a three day fast – with one meal a day of dry bread and black tea or coffee – and a twenty-four hour vigil where you prayed all night in the basilica and then stayed awake – praying, walking, biding time – until the following evening. I also knew that no casual observers, writers, photographers or tourists, were allowed on the island, so if I went, it would be as a pilgrim.

Twice I planned to go, but both days dawned cold and wet and somehow the pleasures of a warm home, good food and company seemed too precious to sacrifice.

Then, for no reason I can think of, I awoke on the morning of my third attempt looking forward to it. I left the house without eating, as pilgrims were supposed to have fasted since midnight, and drove for two and a half hours, through Donegal town to Pettigo, the small border town, where four or five stalls had been set up selling oatcakes and soft drinks – which were all that returning pilgrims were allowed until midnight, when their three days' fast would be over. People were milling around, buying and selling, and the town had a strangely festive air.

After Pettigo the road meandered for several miles through bleak unprepossessing countryside and ended in a car park where people were getting out of coaches, cars and mini-buses, busily gathering their luggage.

I paid my fee at the ticket office and received an instruction leaflet: 'Saint Patrick's Purgatory, Lough Dearg: The Pilgrimage Exercises'. I glanced at it apprehensively as I waited for the boat.

It was the fourth consecutive day of sunshine, and for a bog lake – usually slate dark under overcast skies – the water was surprisingly blue. As we set out, slight waves glanced off the side of the boat, rocking it gently, and in the distance, Station Island, with its basilica and surrounding cluster of buildings, looked almost Venetian. The outboard motor whirred. The motion of the boat was just enough to generate a breeze. I looked across the water at the few scraggy rocks which rose above it. It was hard to believe that at one time a monastic colony had settled on one of these. On another, a clump of stunted Scots pines marked the graves of those who had drowned when the ferry capsized on this same short journey in 1795. Today, the water was as soft and accommodating as a feather pillow; on that occasion it must have been wild and unpredictable, churned into a white-crested swell by sudden lashes of wind. Ninety out of ninety-six pilgrims had been drowned only meters away from the island.

At the reception desk in the women's hostel we were told which rooms were ours. I made my way up two flights of stairs and along a seemingly endless corridor. Most of the rooms slept two; ours slept four, in two blocks of bunks. My roommates were from Limerick: a mother and her two daughters. As the whole weekend had to be spent barefoot we took off our shoes and socks and then put clean sheets on our beds. They told me they had all been before: the mother, Eileen, five times, and her daughters, Sinead and Yvonne, twice.

'It's the vigil that's the hardest,' they assured me. 'The fasting's easy.'

Outside, watching crowds of pilgrims, barefoot and rosary in hand, picking their way painfully through banks of stones, I felt utterly displaced. Most of the people on the island must have been born and grown up in a world where Catholic belief and ritual were as much part of the natural order as day following night and spring leading from winter to summer. I had been told it didn't matter that I wasn't a Catholic, and I was relieved to see that other pilgrims needed to follow instructions for the Station from the leaflet we had been given:

Begin with a visit to the Blessed Sacrament in Saint Patrick's Basilica. Then go to Saint Patrick's Cross, near the basilica: kneel and say one Our Father, one Hail Mary and one Creed. Kiss the Cross.

Streams of pilgrims wandered in and out of the basilica, like the flow of visitors to any great cathedral in the tourist season. But there were no cameras, no guides or guidebooks, and instead of the tourist's brash consumerism, there was a mood of quiet reverence. Joining the crowd, I blessed myself with holy water from the stone font in the portico, genuflected before the Blessed Sacrament and stood for a moment in the cool dark space, then following others outside, I squeezed into the crowd of pilgrims kneeling at Saint Patrick's cross. Everyone was silent for a moment, praying, then one by one they rose and kissed the rusty iron.

At Saint Brigid's Cross, carved on an ancient stone set into the outside basilica wall, you knelt again. Then, having waited your turn in the queue, you stood alone with your back to the cross, and stretching your arms wide, proclaimed: 'I renounce the World, the Flesh and the Devil.'

Standing there, the words on my lips, I felt a disarming solemnity: respect, or perhaps empathy, for the genera- tions of pilgrims, their lives torn apart by temptation they couldn't resist, who had stood in this same spot and before this same sun, this same cross, had vowed from that moment to be strong.

Afterwards it was a relief to walk four times, slowly, round the outside of the basilica, to distance myself from the crowds, to feel the soft breeze blowing up from the lake. In front of me two elderly women wearing track suit bottoms under their skirts, were strolling gently, arms linked, thumbs winding their rosary beads as they silently prayed.

Again we queued: this time for the penitential beds, which are the remains of the beehive cells where early Christian monks ensconced themselves in retreat. Now all that remains are the foundation stones, jagged and protruding from the ground at awkward angles. Each cell or bed is dedicated to a different saint, and you make your way several times round each, kneeling twice, once at the entrance and once at the crucifix in the centre. Every so often someone would lurch in their tracks, wincing, as they mistimed a step or stubbed a toe, and like dominoes others behind would be thrown off their balance.

'It's even worse in the rain,' said the man beside me, 'when the stones are slippery. Sometimes the beds get so waterlogged they have to be mopped out with a sponge and the smell of wet feet would make you want to vomit.'

'I suppose I'm lucky – my first time and a beautiful day like this.'

'Ah, there's none of us lucky until tomorrow.'

The sun was so hot now that the grassy mound with its coils of pilgrims on the penitential beds looked like the site of a holiday attraction. Many of the younger people were dressed in the ubiquitous bright clothes of summer – jeans or shorts and oversized T-shirts emblazoned with mottoes: 'I love Palm Springs' or 'Hard Rock Café'. Others wore sunglasses or visor caps, protecting their noses and eyes.

At Saint Bridget's bed by the bell-tower: Three times round the outside by the right hand, three Our Fathers, three Hail Mary's, One Creed.

It was almost impossible to concentrate simultaneously on the prayers and the layout of stones at my feet. Most of the time the prayers drifted through my mind with the rhythm of a clockwork music box: when I remembered to wind it, they rang out loud and clear, then they slowed down and grew fainter until I eventually realised they'd stopped. Often I'd no idea how many Hail Marys or Lord's Prayers I had said, but as far as I know most people kept count.

Saint Brendan's Bed, Saint Catherine's Bed, Saint Patrick's Bed, Saint Columba's bed… At some point along the way where the path dropped steeply and the smooth stones had become slippery with dust and wear, several people who had finished their three rounds for the day, stood by and, as we approached, reached for us with an outstretched hand or a guiding clasp of the elbow. Already a few people had sprained their ankles or cut themselves. I noticed a nun, her face pale and drawn beneath her veil, her feet streaming with blood.

It occurred to me as I was walking that feet are amongst the intimate parts of the body: intimate in the sense that, in this climate anyway, they are rarely seen and are therefore private, but also in the sense that – more than hands – they give whoever sees them instant access to their owner's character, their way of life, their past. Walking in front of me was a man in his sixties or early seventies, wearing a navy striped Sunday suit. The cuffs of the trousers had been rolled up revealing the zigzag of pinking shears, and beneath them his feet were soap-white with a network of dense blue veins. Three of the nails on each of his feet were black. I felt a wave of pity for him that wasn't my prerogative as silently, head bowed, he carried out his Station.

There were happier feet as well: the immaculate porce-lain feet of a teenager wearing flower-printed culottes; sinuous feet that wrought themselves pliantly over the stones; feet with eye-catchingly red nail varnish; freckled feet, white feet, feet that were stained orange from badly applied fake-tan.

Suddenly a crowd of young men pushed their way past me, breaking the rhythm of my footsteps, violating the silence with their unspoken volume. Afterwards, when their sour sweat had receded, I wondered angrily why they had come.

Then, as I knelt by the crucifix at Saint Patrick's bed, my equanimity returned. Hands reached in from every side, grasping on to the iron cross as people steadied themselves, descending to their knees or rising again when their prayers were said. One old woman leaned heavily down on my shoulder as she painstakingly lowered herself into a space between crouched bodies. Her other hand rested by mine; a naked hand with no watch, rings or bracelets, with nails clipped short and skin pale and loose as though she had just been washing clothes.

And amongst the hands, faces loomed down to kiss the bronze statue of Christ. All around, only centimetres away from my face there were lips with moustaches, painted lips, cracked lips, lips with cold sores, lips that exuded halitosis or garlic or warm cut grass, lips that kissed silently, lips that smacked, lips that left a fine trail of spittle.

Go to the water's edge; stand and say five Our Fathers, five Hail Marys and one Creed; kneel and repeat these prayers.

The view over the lake was soothing after the cramped chaos of the beds. I knelt on one of the flat stones provided. Water lapped the shore gently and a broken rosary lay refracted amongst the pebbles and the reeds.

After the first Station plates and cups clattered and voices swept in waves through the refectory as we gathered for the one meal of the day. We sat at long tables and waitresses distributed plates of steaming white toast or oatcakes and filled and refilled our cups with tea or coffee from pots so big it took both hands to hold them.

Although the tea and coffee had to be taken black, and the toast and oatcakes dry, the meal was reviving and quelled the pain and irritability of hunger. I opted for the homemade oatcakes, dunking one after another into my tea, because I thought they would take longer to digest than the flimsy white bread, but most people found them unpalatable. In fact, I was surprised how fussy people could be despite their obvious hunger. The couple next to me ate only one or two slices of toast each because, they said, they didn't like it dry, and their daughter chewed the moist centres only, discarding the crusts. I couldn't help smiling at an old woman at the next table who was happily shovelling mountains of sugar not only into her tea but on to slice after slice of toast as well.

The man opposite me finished eating and, pushing aside his plate, leaned back expansively as though contemplating an after dinner cigar or a brandy. Then, seeing the waitress, he beckoned her and settled down with another cup of coffee.

'What I like about Lough Dearg,' he said, 'is its levelling effect. People lose their airs and graces. Bricklayers mix with bankers, and neither one feels better because neither one can tell the difference.'

I agreed, appreciating what he was saying, but unable

to prevent myself categorising him as the banker and not the bricklayer.

'They say that Lough Dearg is the middle-class pilgrimage, whereas Croagh Patrick and Knock are more popular with working people. There are more women than men here too – but that's the same at Knock.'

We both looked round to confirm this.

'Your first time, is it?'

'Yes,' I said, wondering how he could tell.

'And yours, Father?' he said to the young Burmese priest on my right.

'It is,' he said in stilted English, adding shyly, 'but it isn't Father, yet – it's just easier for me to wear the collar.'

I couldn't help wondering why this was: whether it made his intentions clear to women, or even to himself, but I didn't ask. The 'banker' was right that, in a sense, we had become to each other like sheep in a flock, but there were still abysses of privacy that kept us apart. For many people, coming here meant confronting some truth about themselves, and possibly admitting it to the priest in confession, but it didn't necessarily mean having it bandied about as casual conversation-filler.

So we talked about missionary work in Burma for a minute or two and then went outside to begin the two more Stations that had to be completed before Night Prayers and Benediction.

*

The shadows were lengthening now, and as the sun's glare receded, the island fell under the calm hush of concentration. When the bell rang, calling us for Mass, it was more of an interruption than a release. Crowds of people poured into the basilica, flooding its sombre interior with colour and noise. The Prior, tall and gaunt in his black cassock, strode about directing stragglers to sparsely filled pews, urging the seated to move along and pack themselves tightly. For a while a harmonium orchestrated the commotion, then there was silence.

I looked around at the faces, serene in concentration, and at the stained-glass colours weakly projected from the evening sun. The Prior, resplendent now in purple, held up the wafer and in a voice heavy with import repeated Christ's words:

Take this, all of you, and eat it: this is my body, which will be given up for you.

A gong quivered eerily; the Prior held up the chalice:

Take this, all of you, and drink from it: this is the cup of my blood, the blood of the new and everlasting covenant. It will be shed for you and for all men so that sins may be forgiven.

A swallow chirruped as it swooped from one window to another across the domed roof of the basilica.

May the body of Christ bring me to everlasting life.

The Prior consumed the wafer.

May the blood of Christ bring me to everlasting life.

He sipped the wine from the chalice.

Afterwards people – with the exception of myself and one or two others – filed to the front of the basilica for Holy Communion.

The day room, where some of us gathered for the long wait until Night Prayers and the beginning of the vigil, reminded me of a harbour terminal before the departure of a delayed cross-channel ferry. We settled ourselves in rows, looking out over the water, watching the sun set and the twilight grow dim. A few people still had the energy for conversation and laughter, but most of us were subdued, our spirits quelled by dread of the long night to come.

I went outside for some fresh air and to fetch my jacket and one or two things I would need for the night. The sky was almost green with the pale luminescence that you see in the desert, and only the evening star was out. I sat on one of the benches; but within seconds swarms of midges had clustered around me, homing in on my bare feet, on my face and hands and the roots of my hair. Irritated to distraction I retreated inside.

'That's always the way. Either it's cold and windy or else it's warm and then you get the midges.' My roommate Eileen rested the Catherine Cookson novel she had been reading face-down on her thigh and rummaged around in her bag. 'You wouldn't know to bring one of these your

first time,' she said, handing me an insect repellent spray,
'Use plenty of it and it will last you the night.'

But despite our precautions, midges billowed like smoke
clouds between the open doors of the basilica and those of
us sitting at the back for Night Prayers and Benediction.
Although the twilight outside was still closer to day than
night, the basilica lights had been lit, suffusing its dank
interior with the warmth of their glow. They generated a
companionship between us that I hadn't noticed at Mass.

The Prior's voice fell silent, a harmonium struck up
and we rose to sing:

> Eyes may close, but you unsleeping,
> Watch by our side:
> Death may come; in love's safe keeping
> Still we abide,
> God of love, all evil quelling,
> Sin forgiving, fear dispelling,
> Stay with us, our hearts indwelling,
> This eventide.

When Benediction was over the great candle that had
been burning all night and day in the basilica was extinguished, marking the end of the vigil for those who had
arrived on the island the day before us. As they hurried
off to bed, their exhausted, sagging faces lightened with

the very knowledge that their long wait for sleep was now over. Another candle was lit, marking the beginning of our own vigil and Christ's presence amongst us.

The Prior spoke again: 'There are many of you here tonight and as many reasons why you have come. Some are seeking God's advice on an important decision, some request His help – with exams, with the illness of a relative, a husband who drinks, a son's long-term unemployment. Others have come to test their faith, to make a difficult confession, to pray for a departed soul – or their own as death approaches.

'We pray to God in many ways, privately at home, collectively in Mass, with our bodies at Lough Dearg. Tonight we offer God our bodies. We pray that He will recognise this sacrifice and grant us our requests.

'In the course of the night, if we listen for His voice, God will speak to us.'

'Because of this, and because our sleeplessness is a *sacrifice* – which of all gifts must be pure and heartfelt – it is crucial that no-one, for a single second, should fall asleep and break the vigil.'

'I'd give my grandmother's pearls to be back in the pub with a glass of Guinness in front of me and a wee goldie beside it.' A look of genuine longing came over the Roscommon man's face. 'And the night's only just beginning.'

He took a packet of Majors out of his pocket, offered me one, and lit up. 'There was a time when you couldn't even smoke.'

He inhaled his cigarette langorously as though it was the one consolation left on earth. Then, exhaling, he contemplated it nestling between his strong nicotine-stained fingers.

'It may kill me in the end, but I'd say I'd be hungry now without it.'

We were sitting in the night shelter, ignoring the Prior's advice to spend five or ten minutes waking ourselves up in the cold air outside, before the night schedule started.

When the bell rang, we reluctantly made our way back to the basilica bundled up in coats and jackets now. The night-time routine consisted of four more Stations, with a break after each one, until Mass at 6.30 in the morning. The Stations were carried out in the basilica this time, not the penitential beds, and the prayers were said out loud led by a succession of pilgrims and clergy, whose voices, amplified from the pulpit, also told us where we should imagine ourselves to be.

Kneel at the entrance to Saint Brigid's bed.

Walk three times round Saint Catherine's bed.

It was a relief after constraining our movements to the cramped confines of the beds, to wander at will through the comparatively spacious basilica. Some people walked round the outside; some strolled up and down the aisle, to the altar rail and back; others climbed the stairs and explored the gallery. For a while exhaustion, boredom, hunger receded with this simple change of scene.

Hail Mary, full of grace, blessed art thou amongst women and blessed is the fruit of thy womb, Jesus.

My eyes fell on two sisters walking up the central aisle as I made my way slowly down the side. I had noticed them before, at the beds and in the refectory. They were in their early twenties, both beautiful. One had the perfect looks of a model: thick auburn hair swept back from symmetrical features unflinching as a photograph, lips painted so red you couldn't help but look. Her sister's hair was black, her face pale and changing with her every fleeting thought and mood. I tried to imagine their lives outside Lough Dearg: actors, dancers, in Dublin, Galway? Earlier, as they had left the refectory, a group of middle-aged traditionalists had muttered, 'Hoors!', then turned their heads for another look.

I believe in God, the Father almighty,
creator of heaven and earth.
I believe in Jesus Christ, his only son, our Lord.
He was conceived by the power of the Holy Spirit
and born of the Virgin Mary.
He suffered under Pontius Pilate,
was crucified, died and was buried...

Prayers flooded the basilica, relentless as waves in a groundswell. Sometimes you were swept along with the surge of voices, but then if your mind started to drift, the words would come tumbling over each other and you felt you were drowning.

Kneel at Saint Brendan's bed, came the drawling amplified voice.

Minutes passed. Then when the rest of us rose to walk on, one man remained with his chin on the altar-rail, blissfully abandoned to sleep.

> *He descended to the dead.*
> *On the third day he rose again.*
> *He ascended into heaven,*
> *and is seated at the right hand of the Father.*
> *He will come again to judge the living and the dead...*

Amongst the bleary faces, the mechanical voices, the bodies that moved slowly, reluctantly, one woman stood out. Her hair was coiled around her head in charcoal-coloured plaits and she was wearing a beige pleated skirt and a cream blouse which she had fastened at the throat with a silver Celtic cross. Watching her, I understood what the Prior had meant when he said that this night should be a sacrifice: that if we loved God enough, this gift, our suffering, would be made unflinchingly. Each time I noticed her, her movements were lithe and alert, her dark eyes aware of the words that most of us now chanted blindly. I imagined her at one time bringing up a family, teaching her children the catechism and saying the Rosary with them at night. They would have left home by now, maybe abandoned their faith in the free-wheeling scepticism of an English or American city. And so her own faith would have deepened: to mitigate God's displeasure with them lest it turn to vengeance, and because, now she was alone, the rhythms of the Church gave her life joy and continuity – the daily Masses, the baptisms, confirmations, marriages, funerals: the warm glow of Christmas and the Nativity; Lent and the desolation of Good Friday; then two days later the church radiant with flowers and sunshine and the beginning of spring ...

> *I believe in the Holy Spirit,*
> *the holy Catholic Church,*
> *the communion of saints,*
> *the forgiveness of sins,*
> *the resurrection of the body*
> *and the life everlasting. Amen*

By the end of the penultimate Station dawn had come and during the break I went down to the pier to watch the light spreading over the water, hoping that the natural progression from night to day could somehow lighten my spirits. But it was a sombre affair: a lustreless gleam that extinguished the stars and then slowly, casually, diluted the darkness. A wind had risen, cold and bitter and scoring the lake like a cracked car windscreen. I shivered and searched the sky for signs of the previous day's warmth, but it was still too soon to distinguish between the grey of emptiness and the solid grey of cloud cover.

By the end of the final Station the sun had still not risen over the hills, but a few pinkish clouds in the east and the pink vapour trail of an inaudible jet announced another clear day. One or two people who had arrived the day before us emerged from the hostels, refreshed from their sleep and dressed in cool summer clothes. I envied their bright-eyed exuberance.

In Mass, wedged comfortably between warm bodies and lulled by the drone of the Prior's voice, it was virtually impossible not to drift off to sleep. Everywhere, eyelids flickered closed, heads drooped helplessly. The Prior reminded us that the vigil was not over until ten at night, and that until then we must constantly guard against sleep. If for a single minute we allowed ourselves to stretch out in the sun, then all would be lost; and if the temptation became too strong, we must walk, keep walking, encourage others to walk.

'I was fine until Mass – I didn't drop off once all night – but it just seemed to go on and on...'

My companion must have been in her eighties. She

was wearing a frayed straw hat, a blue-and-white printed cotton dress that would have been fashionable in the forties, and a black hand-knitted cardigan. Her knees and lower legs were swollen and black with varicose veins. Watching her cumbersome movements as we sat on a bench outside the basilica, I realised that the penitential beds must have given her agony.

'This is my twenty-first time,' she said, with a glimmer of pride. 'I was housekeeper to a priest in County Monaghan for forty years and every other year – the second week in July – we travelled here together. It was such a pleasure, speeding through the summer fields on the train and then on the bus. But he passed away five years ago – God rest his soul. This is my first time alone.' Tears had flooded her eyes.

'I thought about going back to my own people in County Wicklow then. But he needs me. He had a brother – nice man, a schoolteacher – but he was killed in a car crash in America a few years ago. Now he only has me. I visit his grave every evening, summer and winter...'

She was shaking, racked with emotion. I didn't know how to comfort her. I put my hand on her arm and wondered whether so much sadness meant that she and her priest had been lovers.

At the Sacrament of Reconciliation, people made their way, one by one, to the front of the basilica to confess:

not privately in confession booths, but openly kneeling before one of a row of priests in full view of the congregation. As they left the basilica and set foot again on the penitential beds for the final Stations, their outward serenity only half-concealed the brazen exuberance of personal triumph.

I confess to almighty God and to you my brothers and sisters that I have sinned through my own fault, in my thoughts and in my words, in what I have done and in what I have failed to do...

For your penance you will say the Litany of Saints once a day for three days. Now go in peace, my child. Pray for me.

And so, slowly, the day unfolded. For many people the Sacrament of Reconciliation marked a turning point: with confession, fear and guilt had been dissipated and the rest of the pilgrimage was merely a question of waiting. No courage was required, no effort other than that of endurance.

In time the sun rose over the hill. The boats went out as those who had arrived the day before us and had completed their pilgrimage resumed the haphazard contentment of everyday life.

The ceremony for the renewal of the Baptismal Promise, at midday, was a final absolution, as well as a celebration of the symbolic rebirth that followed. Sunshine streamed through the stained-glass windows, splattering the limestone with colour and light. The Prior blessed the baptismal water and the congregation stood.

Do you reject Satan?

I do.

And all his works?

I do.

And all his empty promises?

I do.

God... has given us a new birth by water and the Holy Spirit, and forgiven all our sins. May he also keep us faithful to our Lord Jesus Christ for ever and ever. Amen

And the Baptismal water was scattered about.

Afterwards, we could eat, and the meal once again renewed strength, so the hours that followed seemed shorter, even enjoyable. The wind had increased, whipping up the water, disseminating its chill vapour, but the sheltered side of the island was as warm as a greenhouse. Realising this, people had crammed themselves three abreast onto every available bench. Some were careful to shade their heads with newspapers or knotted handkerchiefs, but most just soaked up the sun, talking or reading, dozing, unaware until later that their faces were burning painfully.

A group of schoolgirls, who had come on a mini-bus from Sligo, started shrieking with laughter, caught up in some multi-sided banter between those on the benches and those on the other side of the walkway, dangling their feet in the lake. It was two months until their exams they had told me earlier, but they had been too busy having fun to focus on their work. Now, either God would notice them here on the island or they'd probably fail.

After a while they too fell silent, their youthful energy spent. One or two persevered with school textbooks or magazines, but most just peeled back their clothes, covered themselves in suntan lotion, and abandoned themselves to the sun.

Gradually the shadows lengthened. At some point during the afternoon I had stopped feeling bored, stopped feeling hungry and tired, stopped desperately wanting to leave the island. I had tried at first to lose myself in the New York excitement of my book, but the words had swum on the page. I had enjoyed conversations: with two lawyers from Belfast and a couple from Dublin. I had walked round the island, again. But in the end I had resigned myself to an animal state of being, letting the day wash over me, mesmerised by the sun's glistening reflection on the water and the way that it stayed put as the waves drifted endlessly through it.

In time the hills on the other side of the lake turned from brown to auburn. We went to Mass. The sun set and the midges returned. We went to Night Prayers and

Benediction. The Vigil candle was extinguished, another was lit, and our day was over.

'What's the first thing you're going to eat at midnight tomorrow?' asked the youngest of my roommates, tantalising her sister, as we lay in our bunks.

'Anything and everything I can lay my hands on,' came the sleepy reply.

'I'm going to go straight to bed as soon as we get home,' said their mother climbing into the bunk above mine. 'I'll set the alarm for midnight, get up, pour myself a gin and tonic and contemplate the possibilities... In the meantime, though, the sleep of the dead.'

But it wasn't. First of all, the schoolgirls in the rooms next to ours started chattering and knocking on the walls. Then when all was quiet and we were eventually drifting off to sleep, someone further down the corridor started screaming:

'Bernadette. Bernadette, for God's sake help me. Bernadette.'

For a while there was silence. Then it came again:

'Jesus Christ, Bernadette, will you help me.'

Doors banged, bare feet pattered in the corridor, voices muttered unintelligibly, and the screaming finally dissolved into the sniffs and sobs of weeping.

After that I couldn't sleep. My mind kept drifting to the time when there was a cave on the island and you had to spend a day and night alone in it after fasting and doing penance for fifteen days. On the morning of the sixteenth day you lay in a coffin, the lid was closed and a Requiem Mass was said for you as though you were dead. Finally, when you must have been distraught with hunger, exhaustion, emotional trauma, the Prior led you to the mouth of the cave and closed the door.

What followed was a journey through purgatory. Chilling accounts still exist of the mental and physical torture that pilgrims endured: their senses were battered with sickening smells, with noise so loud it disoriented the brain, with overwhelming heat followed by bitter, searing cold. Occasionally they caught a glimpse of hell, where sinners floundered in a pit of fire. Then they saw heaven, and clawed their way towards it while demons alternately obstructed them and lured them astray with temptations too hard to resist.

When the Prior finally opened the door, the pilgrim inside was often half-deranged and had to be carried out. Some devoted the rest of their lives to penance: to fasting, prayer and celibacy.

Whatever inspired those stories – bravado, hallucinations, the reality – they made Saint Patrick's Purgatory famous. Pilgrims flocked here from all over Europe: young men to test their mettle; others to undergo purgatory here on earth, so that when they died, they'd be guaranteed instant access to heaven. That was from the twelfth to the fifteenth century, when Europe lost interest.

Sleep eventually flooded my mind. But then doors

started banging again, taps were turned on and off, toilets flushed. I looked at my watch: it was five o'clock – I could hardly believe that people were getting up an hour early to pray before Mass.

But nothing could mar my pleasure in that morning: neither lack of sleep nor excessive sanctimoniousness. We went to Mass, we completed one final Station, hardly caring now if we tripped over stones and bruised or cut our feet. Then we packed our bags and made our way down to the pier.

As we waited for the boat, the sun's warmth grew and the mist evaporated until sky and lake were the same deep blue.

'Would you come again?' asked the man beside me.

'No, I don't think so.' I was watching a young couple, shod now, and holding hands as they made their way jauntily down to the pier. 'No. Once was enough.'

'They say the island "calls", you know. I had no intention of coming. Then six years ago my wife died. That was the first time – not that she needed it. But it helped, it really helped. I've been back three times since. It's the challenge. Nothing can beat that feeling – the sense of achievement – when you finally step on that boat ...'

In the car park, doors slammed and a line of traffic made its way slowly towards the road.

It occurred to me as I was driving, that pilgrims must

have passed this way for fifteen hundred years: maybe more. In all probability Lough Dearg was a Celtic place of worship long before Saint Patrick and Christianity came to Ireland. Then like so many stone formations and sacred wells that were circled in the same way as the beds, it was incorporated into the Christian tradition to ease the path of conversion.

In the seventeenth century, as part of the Penal Laws, the British government banned communal worship and for years the shores of the lake were patrolled, the boats and pier were burned and the buildings on the island were razed to the ground. But the Stations were still carried out at secret places on the mainland and, through it all, the tradition survived.

I wound down the window and felt the cool breeze blow through the car. On either side of the road tufts of cotton grass, catching the sunlight, flickered against the dark brown of the bog. There was no other traffic on the road.

AN EIGHTEEN FOOT PUNT

There had been a storm two days before, force nine gales and great driving seas. The boat, an eighteen-foot punt, had been winched high up the slip, beyond the lashing of breakers and spray, to where green grass laid claim to the crumbling concrete. Seamus and Diarmaid, wearing oilskins and wellingtons, guided her down, one on either side, straining to keep her upright, to keep their footing on the lichen and weed, as another brother, Thomas, operated the winch, lowering her gradually, foot by foot. Eventually the boat slithered in with a splash. Seamus waded in after her and, with a steadying hand on the bow, climbed aboard.

The wind had dropped almost completely during the night and the early forecast had been good, with the storm now away out over the North Sea. It was a sultry morning; damp, misty and still.

Seamus started the outboard and manoeuvred the boat to the front of the pier. When he was close enough he threw up a rope to Thomas who moored her to a rusty post. The boat secure, Thomas started to pass down the lobster pots that they had brought in as the sky grew dark with the storm, while Diarmaid filled a fish box with bait from a barrel of brine at the back of the pier. As he carried it down the slippery steps to the water's edge the smell of rotten fish rose behind him, rank and nauseating.

There were three of us in the boat as she set out across the bay: Seamus was standing at the stern, looking ahead towards the open sea, contemplating the hours to come, as with one hand lightly on the tiller, he guided her through the harbour. Diarmaid, protected by his oilskins and a pair of work gloves, was sitting astride one of the seats cutting up bait. Offal and putrid liquid from the gurnards, *byan*, pollack and crabs spilled across the seat in front of him, his chopping board. Every so often he would wipe it down and sluice it with sea water. I was sitting on the small seat at the bow, gliding backwards.

The boat had been freshly painted in spring – grey with a black trim – but already, by mid-July, her colour and gloss had faded. Two knives, one long one short, both honed to a shining razor sharpness, were slotted by their blades through the curved boards of the hull. Between Diarmaid and Seamus was a ramshackle pile of lobster pots: between Diarmaid and myself the box of bait, a bailer, a rope, a bucket made from a sawn-off jerry-can, and a wooden tomato box. There were no life jackets or safety equipment on board: only the wooden oars lying diagonally across the gunwale. There were three of them not two, in case one was lost overboard, leaving the other as useless as a single bicycle pedal.

'There was a time,' said Seamus, watching me looking around, 'when they used to keep holy water on the boats and every time they went out they'd sprinkle it about, blessing them.'

When Seamus was in his early twenties he had spent a year working in Manchester. He hated it. Then he had driven a digger for a construction company in Galway. That lasted four months. Diarmaid, at seventeen, was the youngest of the three brothers. He too had worked in England, as a builder's labourer in Neasden, until the job finished a few months ago. He didn't want to go back to England, but the fishing was just a summer job. Every year either he or Thomas, or sometimes both, came back to help Seamus, glad of the chance to leave England and the city, and to spend the summer at home.

The boat had left the harbour now and was following the coast south-west. In the open sea her progress was slower as she climbed each wave, dipped, righted herself, and was rocked again. White ribbons of foam trailed down the rocks off the shore as the waves swept over them and subsided, lurching back with the undertow.

'That's a big swell the day,' Seamus commented, half to himself: then louder, to me, 'A ground sea like that is the worst condition for fishing.'

'Worse than the wind, or fog?'

'Oh aye. If the wind's getting up or a storm's on the way, they'd tell you about it on the forecast. And these days they're nearly always right. But with a ground sea, the only way you'd know, until you're out in it, is when you see the isobars piled almost on top of each other away out over the Bay of Biscay.'

The sound of the outboard dropped to a purr as the boat slowed down, approaching a buoy. Diarmaid put aside the bait he was cutting, slotted the knife safely in place with the other one, and as the boat drew up alongside the buoy, leaned over and lunged for the rope beneath it. The resistance of the lobster pot, lying on the bottom, stopped the boat short, and bracing his feet on the slippery boards, Diarmaid hauled vertically. When the pot eventually surfaced, it was empty.

Seamus had once told me that he used to make the lobster pots himself. The design was simple enough: a rectangle of wooden boards weighted down with concrete, three lengths of plastic piping bent into an arch and covered with net, and an entrance made from a bottomless flowerpot. There was a time, he said, when all the pots had been round, following the design of the first pots ever seen in this part of the country. Those had been French, belonging to a boat that regularly fished these waters, filling its hold with lobsters and taking them all the way back to France, 'as if they hadn't enough on their own coast'.

Diarmaid cracked the shell of a crab so the meat was more accessible and attached that and a fish head to the inside of the pot as bait. Then he threw the pot as far as he could away from the boat. As it started to sink, he fed the rope after it and finally the buoy.

The boat started up again.

A few minutes later Seamus made some comment and pointed out to sea. It was hard to hear what he was saying above the noise of the engine and the waves. He said it again, louder, 'You see that disturbance in the water over there, Monica?'

I looked across and at first I saw nothing, just the grey-green sea shading into the mist. Then I noticed a patch of water as faintly white as saliva where the waves seemed to be breaking for no reason at all.

'That's Dunleavy's *buillig*,' he explained. 'It's a submerged rock. Sometimes at high tide you'd hardly know it was there.'

A pair of fulmars that had been following the boat since we left the harbour dived simultaneously after a tangle of guts that Diarmaid had thrown overboard. But they were too late: the guts sank and the birds picked themselves dexterously out of the water, turned, and swooped low over the boat. For a moment they hovered, visibly contemplating the box of bait, then, slowly, they glided away.

'*Seabhac cac an faoileós*,' said Seamus dismissively.

'What?'

'*Seabhac cac an faoileós*,' he repeated. 'It means shit-eating birds – they'd eat anything.'

At the next buoy it was Seamus's turn to haul, but the pot refused to budge. Diarmaid put aside his knife and both of them pulled with all of their strength. Still the pot wouldn't yield. Seamus had told me earlier that if the pots are left out during a storm they can be dragged about by the swell and become so entangled in weed and rocks that all you can do is leave them there. But this time at least, the pot, almost imperceptibly at first, started to shift. Then eventually it was free. As Seamus lifted it out of the water, we could tell there was a lobster in it by the scrabbling sound, like a dog's claws on vinyl.

When the pot was safely on board, Diarmaid reached inside and, with his gloved hand, gripped the lobster firmly by the back and lifted it out. It was a big one – nearly a foot long. He set it down carefully and turned to re-bait the pot. For a while the lobster clattered and creaked at my feet, flicking its articulated shell tail against the bottom of the boat. Then it settled down, clutching Seamus's discarded jacket with claws as long as its body and emitting a deep cicada like grinding.

A few minutes later the pot splashed back into the water and Diarmaid turned his attention to the lobster. Again he held it by the back, explaining that that way it could neither reach your hand with its claws nor trap your fingers in the joints of its tail if it decided to flick it. As he picked it up, the lobster flailed aggressively, and holding the body between his knees, Diarmaid wedged his forearm lengthwise between its claws, pinning them back. For a moment the pincers opened and closed round thin air. Then Diarmaid bound first one set, then the other, with elastic bands.

'They beat each other up,' he explained, 'Sometimes even kill each other.'

He checked that the bands were tight enough, then put the lobster carefully into the tomato box at my feet.

'You see that wee bay over there, Monica?' said Seamus. He was pointing to a pale semi-circular beach at the foot of the cliffs. 'They say that a Spanish galleon was shipwrecked there during the Armada.'

He paused, taking another cigarette from his packet, lighting it. 'They say there's another bay – they call it the Spaniard's Bay – away on round the coast, where a Spanish sailor was washed up in one of the worst storms ever known. A couple of fishermen found him and went straight back for the priest – in those days they wouldn't have handled a drowned body themselves. So the priest arrived and gave him his blessings, but just as he was finishing the final prayer the Spaniard raised his head and sat up. When he realised what had happened he was so grateful that he gave the priest his solid gold belt and told him to build churches with it. You can still see the remains of those churches today. They call them the Spanish churches.'

'Do you believe that?' said Diarmaid doubtfully.

Seamus shrugged. 'It's folklore. But there *were* a lot of Spanish boats went down around here. That's why so many of us have black hair and dark complexions.'

'I thought that was all the sun we get.'

Slowly the boat worked its way round the coast: past the Quiet Strand, where despite the drizzle, one or two holiday-makers were bathing; past An Coirnéal, the smoothly rounded corner rock at the mouth of the bay; past An Chlock Mhor, the big boulder, which according to legend had once been hurled down from the cliffs; past Carraig na Bdroighean, tall and pyramid-shaped and densely clustered with cormorants and shags, some fidgeting and spreading their wings to dry, others staring quietly out to sea. Every so often we'd slow down for Diarmaid to throw out one of the pots we had brought with us, now baited and ready, or we'd stop at a buoy while either Seamus or Diarmaid hauled.

At one point we had a long stretch of good luck, a succession of pots coming up with two or even three lobsters. Then for half an hour there was nothing: just the pots, empty, or with only their sodden, disintegrating bait.

'You'll never guess what they call this place,' said

Seamus, as we drifted up to a cliff where the air felt dank and a strange wind blew like the draught from an open window in a long-unoccupied house. 'The Half-Mile Cliff.'

I looked up at the sheer rock; at the waterfall virtually somersaulting over itself, and the trails of white, like streamers, beneath ledges where sea-birds were nesting. As I was watching, a kittiwake glided towards the cliff, then at the last minute, catching the air stream, rose almost vertically, twenty or thirty feet, to land by its mate.

Occasionally the pots seemed dangerously close to the rocks as the boat lurched unpredictably in the dark waters under the cliff. Seamus once told me that fear is something that has to be learned. There are levels of fear and unless you're given a yardstick you won't know how to pitch your reactions or where your threshold should be. When Seamus was learning to fish his father had taken him out in a sea much rougher than this. One of the pots had been dragged by the swell right up to the rocks and Seamus was terrified as the boat plunged this way and that, then nose-dived off course on the crest of a wave.

'Well,' said his father, 'Will we try for it again or will we leave it?'

It wasn't until much later that Seamus realised his father had been almost as scared as was; but he had needed to test his son's respect for the sea before he could let him out on his own.

Suddenly as we turned back in the direction of the harbour, Seamus pointed to something that looked like a fish being swept about at the top of a net. Diarmaid and I both looked over: the fish was only exposed for a few seconds at a time, before being doused by the waves and lost from sight. But it was definitely a salmon, a big one, and it was definitely still alive. For a minute the two of them considered what they should do: it wasn't their net, yet there was little doubt that a fish as visible as that, if left, would be snatched away in no time by seals or birds. Seamus decided to go in after it.

I was worried, as he manoeuvred the boat alongside the net, that the sea would unbalance her, tossing her too close to the net, fouling the propeller, or into the rocks only yards ahead. Diarmaid and I sat perfectly still, watching helplessly, as Seamus leaned out and reached for the top of the net. When he caught hold of it, he gradually fed it from one hand to the other, pulling the boat towards the salmon. The boat rocked and lurched, making it difficult for him to stay on his feet let alone grab hold of the floundering fish. Luckily it wasn't too deeply entangled, and Seamus was able to virtually lift it out of the water and onto the boat.

We were all relieved to pull out into clear water, away from the rocks and the net. The salmon was a beauty; its flesh full and firm under rippling silver scales. Seamus and Diarmaid both seemed pleased: finding the salmon was lucky – ten minutes earlier it probably wasn't there, ten minutes later it would almost certainly have gone.

For a while we were quiet, lost in our separate thoughts. The motion of the boat had no regular rhythm, unlike a bigger boat which would have rolled and pitched more predictably. But it was a pleasure to be so much part of the sea.

When I looked up I realised that Seamus was asking me something: 'Would you like to buy the salmon, Monica?'

'I'd love to.'

So he explained that he could neither keep it himself, nor sell it and keep the money, because it wasn't his fish. If I wanted to buy it he would reimburse the owner; if not he would take him his fish.

At first I was surprised by Seamus's morality, but as I got to know him better I began to understand. He once told me about a half-decker that had approached him too close as he was shooting his salmon nets. He had waved his arms and shouted but the boat had carried on, cutting right through his net. Seamus was furious and had sworn at the top of his voice, but although the crew must have both seen and heard him, they never looked back. Then, a few months later, Seamus heard that the owner of the boat, faced with ruinous debt, had sold up. Strangely, it was the only boat for miles around which, in that notoriously prolific season, had landed virtually nothing.

The chances are, of course, it was merely coincidence,

but who was to say for sure? To Seamus it was tempting fate to cheat other fishermen, likewise to fish for the money alone, with no feeling for the skill, learning, hard work and experience – in fact the whole way of life – that make up the trade.

Other fishermen felt the same. Even those who were known crooks on land wouldn't dice, in that way, with the sea. Some even had stories of boats that had wronged them going down only days afterwards.

There were exceptions: several years previously there was a lot of money to be made from salmon fishing, but the industry was strictly regulated. It was illegal to fish outside the short season, and on Sundays the nets had to be less than a prescribed length and breadth, with mesh wide enough for the young fish to escape. Some fishermen had felt the restrictions were too tight, and whether in protest or out of sheer greed, they rebelled. I once heard of a patrol boat that had approached a half-decker from one of the bigger ports along the coast. When it drew up the fishermen poured petrol over the officers, lit a match, and asked if they were coming on board or if they were going home instead.

The same strict rules still governed salmon fishing. Equipment was regularly confiscated, fines imposed – but the rewards were not so great, mainly because of competition from farmed salmon. Seamus said he no longer bothered; it wasn't worth his while. But there was a time when he was out almost all day every day, or as often as the weather allowed, for the entire season. Usually he would shoot the nets at dawn, perpendicular to the shore across the path of the salmon as they headed towards the estuaries and rivers. The net would drift with the current and for hours Seamus would watch the corks at regular intervals along its length. When one sank he knew there was a salmon beneath it and all he had to do was lift that one section of net. Sometimes, hour after hour, until dusk was falling, not a single cork would sink.

'One day,' said Seamus when he was telling me this. 'A baby dolphin got caught in the net. It was tangled up badly and I was doing my best to release it when I noticed two adult dolphins watching from some distance. Suddenly it seemed so important that the young one didn't get hurt. I worked away for a long time. Eventually, when I put it back in the water, I was afraid it wouldn't be able to swim. But seconds later it dived away through the waves with the two adults beside it. That was worth twenty salmon to me.'

The drizzle had turned into more persistent rain and this time as we passed the Quiet Strand, there was no one swimming, no one playing or walking on the beach.

The boat slowed down as we approached another buoy. At first I assumed it was a lobster pot but when Diarmaid started to haul, a stone weight came up and I realised it must be a net. As soon as he could reach, Seamus took the top, with the floats, while Diarmaid took the weighted bottom end. This way, as they hauled, the flimsy nylon mesh fell into neat folds at their feet. Occasionally there was a tangled knot of seaweed and they would have to stop and painstakingly unravel it. There were crabs and any number of *byan,* but not a single crayfish, which was what the net was intended for.

Diarmaid shook his head despairingly: 'We should never have brought a black-haired woman on the boat.'

I'd always heard it was red-heads who brought bad luck. In the past, people had told me, a fisherman wouldn't put to sea if he had passed a red-haired woman between his home and his boat. And he certainly wouldn't marry one, or even flirt with one. But when I pointed this out, they both insisted:

'No, it's the black-haired women are the worst.'

The boat pulled away and Seamus and Diarmaid threw the buoy overboard and dropped the heavy stone weight, then as the boat gathered speed they paid out the net, casually picking up a strand every so often, so it more or less unfurled itself.

We passed the entrance to the harbour, continuing up the coast towards the island with its row of derelict houses and the remains of the old school. Seamus said it must have been a hard life for them there, especially the women, being battered in winter by gales and heavy seas, and cut off from the mainland for weeks on end. It was the fishing that had supported them there, but as the industry became more mechanised and focused in the big ports, their livelihood dwindled and, one after another, they abandoned the island.

In Seamus's memory there had been two terrible accidents off the island. Both had involved trawlers, maybe sixty foot or more, and both had gone down in calm seas, just run aground, probably because the skipper, or whoever was on watch at the time, was exhausted, having worked all day and night, as trawlermen were still expected to do, and had fallen asleep. In one of the accidents the entire crew, thirteen or fourteen men, had been lost. In the other there was one survivor.

'How many will there be in this one, Monica?' Seamus asked as he stopped to haul another net.

'Seven,' I decided.

'Seven! If there's seven in it we'll want you with us every day.'

He lifted the stone weight onto the boat. Then seconds later the first cray appeared: a tangled mass of legs, claws, tail and feelers, tightly parcelled in the nylon mesh. Very carefully, he began to unravel it, leaving the rest of the net draping the boat, tilting her slightly as she rose and fell with the drift of the waves. It was a delicate job: the antennae especially were brittle and hard to bend free of the net, and if they snapped at the base the cray usually died and certainly couldn't be sold. But in time Seamus worked it out backwards, the antennae last, and set it down on the floor of the boat. It was bigger than the lobsters, more surreal, and worth over twice as much.

Then as soon as he started to haul again a second cray appeared. This one he set aside for the time being and carried on hauling. Seconds later a third one surfaced. I think by then we all half expected four more, to make up the seven, but that was the last. Afterwards it was mainly crabs and dog fish, with a few gurnards and one or two pollack.

Sometimes as Seamus and Diarmaid were hauling they threw over a clump of weed for me to untangle, or a fish, and when the whole net was on board all three of us worked at clearing it. Apart from the crayfish, which Seamus and Diarmaid dealt with, the *byan* were the hardest to extract, flapping and writhing and tearing my hands with inch long spikes on their undersides and dorsal fins. Sometimes they were so tightly enmeshed I was convinced that either the fish or the net would have to be cut, but if I squeezed them out backwards, scraping the tight mesh over the body, the open gills, the head and bulging eyes, they always came out in the end. The crabs too could be awkward, fast and surprisingly strong as they moved to grab hold of your hand; and the dogfish, more common in the nets that anything else, yet worth-less. All fishermen hated them, for fouling up the nets and because somehow they made their flesh crawl with their half-closed eyes and doggish leer and skin as rough as sandpaper that burned your hand with a single flick of their tails.

The coast was more rugged here than on the other side of the harbour, with outcrops of rock of all shapes and sizes scattered about at the foot of the cliffs. From where we were we could see most of the village: a line of houses, all orientated towards the sea, each with its strip of land, stretching the five hundred or so meters down to the shore. At one point Seamus pointed to a cave that was, he said, the mouth of a blow hole, which only worked in exceptionally stormy seas. It was known as McKeown's Gun, and for a while we all wondered who McKeown had been. Then he pointed out the cliff where a climber had fallen. The helicopter, which in those days came from Dublin, had to stop on the way to refuel, and took five hours to arrive. When the unconscious climber finally got to the hospital, the doctor shook his head: 'Ah, they're a long way out there,' implying that the delay had probably cost him his life.

I don't know how many pots Seamus and Diarmaid hauled that day, how many cray nets. We had been out over three hours and had caught six lobsters and three crayfish. One of the nets had been badly dragged about in the storm and came up with nothing but weed and a single mangled pollack. Another contained a good-sized cray which Seamus instinctively knew to be dead. He disentangled it silently – his face closed off in a way I'd never seen – and threw it into the sea. Afterwards he explained that at this time of year the crays shed their shells and until the new one has hardened they're as soft as human flesh. More than anything he hated to see one killed by the net, as this one had been. But, unfortunately, this the only realistic way of fishing them.

In the final net there was a small cray, which Seamus measured with a plastic guage and threw back, and amongst the usual collection of fish and weed, a sea cucumber, which he said was called a 'sea turd' in Irish, and a John Dory.

'Why's it called a John Dory?' Diarmaid asked.

No one knew the answer.

'What's it called in Irish?'

Seamus didn't know. He once told me that when they were getting ready to go out in the boat two men from the North came over and told them that, with a traditional occupation like theirs, they ought to be speaking Irish, maintaining their culture and heritage. The remark had annoyed him intensely.

'There was a time when they thought the Dory was poisonous. Plenty of people still wouldn't touch them.'

'It's one of my favourite fish.'

'You see that black mark there behind the gill?' He picked up the John Dory to show us the same spot on the other side. 'They call that Saint Peter's mark. It's where

Saint Peter left his thumb and finger print when he caught the fish in the Sea of Galilee and passed it to Jesus. It's like the cross on the donkey's back, from when it carried Jesus to be born in Bethlehem.'

We were heading back towards the harbour now.

'You know it changes colour according to what's beside it. It's camouflaged.'

The John Dory, where it was lying on the floor of the boat, was mottled in zebra stripes of olive green and off white. Diarmaid reached for some seaweed and threw it on top of it. The two of us watched. Gradually the formation of mottles changed as the dark green spread. He took way the seaweed and replaced it with Seamus's yellow jacket. Every few minutes we looked again. It was hard to tell if we imagined it, but it did seem predominantly light.

'I wonder if it goes on changing when it's dead.' The fish was hardly moving now, although the gills and gaping mouth pumped methodically.

For some time the two of us experimented. Seamus was looking ahead, lost in his own thoughts. He lit another cigarette. The sea was slightly calmer as we entered the bay and dark green in the shadow of the surrounding cliffs. A pair of herring gulls looked imperiously down on us from the top of a tall solitary rock as we glided into the harbour.

The boat drew up at a buoy and Seamus pulled in a

heavy wooden box. As it broke the surface we could hear the familiar sound of lobsters scrabbling about inside and see them in between the slats. Without bringing the box into the boat Seamus untied the lid and lifted it off. Then one by one, he picked up the lobsters that were in the boat, checked the rubber bands were tight enough and put them away with the others. The crayfish had a separate box. Before he put them in, Seamus trimmed their claws with a sharp knife and put a little nick the joint, severing the ligament, so they couldn't fight.

'Give that man the fingers will you someone.'

I hadn't noticed that a tourist was watching through a pair of binoculars from the top of the pier. Seamus said there was nearly always someone there with a camera or binoculars. Sometimes he didn't mind. But occasionally, when they'd had a bad day, it was just too much to have an anonymous face leering at them through a camera lens as they unloaded the boat.

Seamus dropped the box of crays back into the sea. Every Friday the agent from Galway came to collect them. Prices varied from year to year and even within a single season following fluctuations in the market, both locally and abroad. The agent drove on up the county, stopping at various ports along the way, and then took the crays and lobsters back to Galway, from where they were shipped to France.

Slowly, we cut across the harbour towards the pier.

Diarmaid was already tidying the boat, bailing out the accumulated water that was sloshing about at our feet, gathering up the seaweed and throwing it overboard. For the time being he put all the fish together in one box, throwing the fresh gurnards, pollack, *byan,* John Dory and crab bodies on top of the morning's unused bait. Only the salmon he kept separate – for fear of tainting it – and the crab toes which he collected in a carrier bag. Sometimes he sold these to one of the restaurants in town, but more often he gave some to friends and neighbours and he and his family ate the rest, either boiled in a big pot, or thrown into the embers and roasted.

Diarmaid stepped out onto the green slime at the bottom of the steps and went to moor the boat. In several trips everything was unloaded and set down on the concrete. As Seamus gutted the first pollack, seagulls gathered overhead, and when he threw a handful of offal into the water they jostled for it in a sudden flurry of wingbeats. Seamus's children loved pollack, and he kept all he caught – filleting, skinning and freezing it – mainly for them. The John Dory he gave to me, refusing my offer of payment. And the salmon was mine too, as we had arranged. The rest of the fish he and Diarmaid carried to the back of the pier and poured into the barrel of brine with the bait. There was no market for it. At harvest time they laid nets especially for *byan,* which they cured in batches to sell to local shops where 'country people' bought them. But out of season one or two were neither here nor there.

We set out for our separate homes: Diarmaid's and Seamus's nearby, mine some distance away. When the two of them had had something to eat and a bit of a rest they'd go out again, making a similar trip in the evening. But I didn't ask them to take me.

There were other times though. Once in the course of an almost Mediterranean heat-wave they told me to meet them at six the next morning. When I arrived at the pier the sky was dull with haze or cloud and a cold north-west wind was blowing in from the sea. It occurred to me that maybe the weather had broken and the wind was too strong to go out. But then Seamus arrived and said the weather forecast was good and the change wasn't due till the following day. Soon afterwards Diarmaid appeared at the top of the steps.

'I suppose *you* thought it was too windy, as well.' Seamus teased him.

But judging by his rumpled hair and T-shirt and the bleary look in his eyes, he was suffering the after effects of Friday night in the pub.

Outside the harbour the boat leap-frogged the waves, throwing back sudden drenchings of spray as she sank into a trough, wrong-footed, and the following wave came crash-splattering over her bow. Gradually the sun came up, orientated low from the land to the sea, so it shone through a hole in the rocks, then an arch, then, as we rounded the corner, in shafts from the cliffs, emphasising in changes of grey their distance and height as they rose progressively up to the Half-Mile Cliff and beyond.

In time the heat of the sun started scorching our skin. Seamus said it was my responsibility to make sure the lobsters and crays were kept cool and moist. He slowed down the boat so I could gather a handful of weed to cover them, and then every so often, as they shifted about, I rearranged it and sloshed them with sea-water that I had scooped up in the bucket. The crays especially were vulnerable; if the exposed flesh on the underside, where the tail joins the body, dried out, they wouldn't survive.

Everyone knew that fishermen were cagey about how many fish they caught. If the catch was particularly good or particularly bad, most would modify their result for reasons of modesty, pride, or whatever superstition. So all I can say is that that morning we were lucky: pot after pot came up with at least one lobster, and more than a few of the nets were bristling with crayfish. I don't even know how many there were at the end, but I do know that when Seamus and Diarmaid tied up the boat they both seemed especially pleased.

Another day Seamus's six-year-old son Hughie came out with us. He loved the boat. Sometimes Seamus let him hold the tiller and steer her or put her into gear and start her up. And he loved the fish we caught, just fingering them at first, then picking them up and feeling the sinewy bodies and the smooth slippery texture of the fins and tails. When Seamus was busy with a net, Hughie would sit quietly, lost in his own world, watching the changing cartoon-faces the fish pulled as he stuck his fingers into their mouths or gills and wiggled them round.

Hughie was looking forward to his fifteenth birthday when Seamus had promised he would take him out every day and teach him to fish. It was the same age that Seamus had started to learn with his father. The two of them had fished together for over twenty years and then when Seamus's father retired, several years ago, he never went out in the boat again, never even went down to the pier.

In those days, and before, in the time of Seamus's grandfather, most of the families in the village owned a boat. Then it was mainly herring they fished. There were four men to a boat, Seamus explained, yawls, they called them; they were like punts but with two bows. In spring and early summer, when the herring were in, one man would stand on the cliffs watching for dark brown patches in the sea, which were shoals of them just under the surface. When he spotted one he'd shout to a second man, who staked one end of the net to the shore, while the boat, with the rest of the net, encircled the shoal. The net was then hauled from the shore. Ring netting it was called.

As Seamus was telling me this I imagined the pier in those times: continually busy, with the old iron oil lamps lit for the salmon boats which could only go out at night because, before the arrival of clear nylon, the nets could be seen by the fish, if they were set in the daytime.

Now only two families owned boats, and Seamus doubted there was the livelihood for more. The herring were all fished by pair trawlers from the big ports around the coast, and salmon and lobster were becoming scarcer by the year.

At the end of the summer Seamus winched the boat to the top of the slip, upturned it, and tied it down with rope, weighted with stones.

The next time I saw him was a stormy day in October. He was digging potatoes in the small plot in front of his house. I noticed he had shaved off his beard and his suntan had faded. He told me that Diarmaid hadn't gone back to England but had found a job in one of the few craft shops that stayed open all year, selling Donegal sweaters and tweed caps to tourists. As for himself, he was working in the fish-canning factory several miles away, as he always did in the winter. I couldn't help thinking that canning mackerel on a production line was a poor exchange for the life he was leading in summer. But Seamus said all

city people love the boat because it's so different from
what they're used to. He liked fishing too – otherwise
he wouldn't do it – but it was hard work, and it could
be boring and lonely and was almost always stressful.
Anyway, he said, in his heart he was a winter person. By
August the summer sickened him – the heat, the long
days and bright light, the *excess* of it.

MISSING YOU

Black smoke surged from the chimney of the parochial house before being snatched by the wind, swept horizontally and dissipated into the iron-grey sky. The door opened and the priest stepped onto the tarmacadamed drive. Standing back several yards from the house he shielded his face from a squall of hailstones and looked up. A flame erupted, as sudden as vomit, and whorls of smoke billowed gently up through the roof.

Inside the house, where I had been chatting with the priest, the hall was filled with a fine veil of smoke and the smell of burning dust and soot. In the parlour the smoke was thicker and yellowish-brown, the smell more acrid. A coal fire was burning brightly in the grate and every so often a gust of smoke would be belched backwards engulfing the flames, the cast-iron fireplace, the Victorian porcelain tiles. Fanned by the draught between the open front door and the gale blowing outside, the flames in the chimney-breast roared like an underground train.

The priest, unruffled, said that he had seen a great many chimney fires in his time and was confident that this one would burn itself out. But just to be sure he called the fire brigade.

Soon afterwards the siren sounded at the fire station across the road from the bottom of the priest's garden. As we stood outside his door we could see the cars approaching as the firemen were summoned from their homes in different parts of the valley, and then watch the big fire station doors open as the men hurried inside and scrambled into their oilskins, wellingtons and helmets.

The fire station had been officially opened just a few months previously by the Minister of State for the Gaeltacht. The whole village had been decorated with bunting and only minutes before the ceremony was due to begin the final touches were still being added to the red 'Fire Station' sign on the gable wall and the double yellow no-parking lines in the forecourt. When everything was ready a crowd of people gathered round, speeches were made and the red converted Land Rover was blessed by the Bishop and taken out for a spin. That week there was a photograph in the Donegal Democrat and a few paragraphs praising the local people who had raised some of the money needed to set up the fire service through lotteries, bazaars and discos.

Within minutes the red fire engine came clattering up the drive. The firemen greeted the priest and joined him outside the door, discussing the situation and what should be done. Almost all of them had seen the smoke and

flames and had been on their way before the priest had
even raised the alarm. In fact, because the parochial house
was situated on a hill and was taller than most of the other
buildings, it was possible that everyone in the valley and
the surrounding hills knew that the priest's chimney was
on fire well before he did himself.

The firemen agreed there was no real cause for
alarm. Although smoke was still drifting up through the
slate roof, the plume above the chimney was probably
less dense than before, the eruptions of fire slightly less
frequent. However, since they were here, the firemen
set about their routine. They raked and stifled the coals
in the grate; checked that the fire hadn't burst from
the chimney into the adjoining bedroom upstairs;
connected their hose to the mains water supply, and
with a certain amount of help from the priest, who had
been a fisherman before he was ordained and still had
the strength of his former profession, assembled their
folding ladders and put them up against the back wall
of the house.

A dark cloud passed overhead releasing a whiplash of
hailstones. That morning there had been snow on the
ground and the forecast was for continuing gales with the
possibility of blizzards. The postman, now in his other,
fireman's, uniform, blew on his bare hands, and with a
wry smile, set foot on the first rung of the ladder.

An hour later we were all sitting in the warmth of

the range in the priest's kitchen, eating porter cake and drinking tea and large measures of brandy. The firemen were still wearing oilskins, but their helmets were now on their laps or on the floor beside their chairs. The brandy after the cold and the lashing of the wind and hail was illuminating their eyes and flushing their faces. Everyone was in good spirits: discussing how the fire had started, how they'd put it out, how efficient their equipment had been.

'I'll tell you one thing though,' said the postman when there was a lull in the conversation. 'I wouldn't want to do that every day.'

'No, but it was a grand way of getting the chimney cleaned.'

It was. But the price was still being paid by the priest's housekeeper who, in rubber gloves and an apron, was on her knees mopping up the black sludge that had been blasted down the chimney by the hose and was welling over the hearth and seeping slowly into the carpet. And then when that had been done she'd have to start on the soot that had settled all over the room – on the curtains, the wallpaper, the glass-fronted bookcase, the framed photographs of former parish priests and school choirs – covering everything like a fine layer of black snow.

That night in Mass the priest praised the pleasures of a convivial drink at this time of year, but warned of the potentially devastating effects on family and community of excessive indulgence in alcohol.

As Christmas approached, decorations appeared in one house after another. Almost always something bright or seasonal would be placed in the window, so that together with a crucifix or a statue of the Virgin, it made a statement to visitors and passers-by, even at night, about the nature of the house and those who lived in it. And in the early evening, when the lights were on but the curtains not yet drawn, you could look into big picture windows and see a string of Christmas cards or tinsel stretched from one wall to another and a Christmas tree festooned with lights and angels' hair and reflective balls that dangled, glittering, from every branch.

For days the gales hardly let up. The roar of the sea could be heard all over the valley as huge waves rolled in, crashing over the rocks and splattering the shore with great downpours of spray. One day when the wind was south-westerly it shunted the breaking waves right over the island with its lighthouse and several derelict houses; then when it veered west, enhancing the incoming spring tide, people thought the estuary would overflow, flooding the plain and the few low-lying houses that had once before been awash with sea water.

Then, as the forecast predicted, the blizzards came. In the valley the snow soon melted, but in the mountains it settled patchily, half-covering clumps of rushes and heather and heaps of turf left stacked by the roadside since summer. Sheep, damp and bedraggled, clung to the shelter of stone walls and outcrops of rock as the wind slewed the snow in dense sheets over the bog. Not many people lived up there: a few sheep farmers. Many of them were bachelors, living in isolated houses on their own or with an unmarried brother or sister or an aging parent, speaking Irish amongst themselves, and coming to town only rarely for a Mass or a funeral, then spending the rest of the day in the bar.

In Keaney's the turf fire was blazing. Light from the single naked bulb glistened cheerfully on the engraved mirrors advertising Jameson's and Guinness, and on the rows of glasses and bottles behind the bar. Through the hatch on the side of the counter we could just see into the lounge where a group of women were sitting by the range. Here in the public bar it was mainly men. Two of the older ones were huddled together talking intimately as though, mellowed by whiskey and seasonal goodwill, they were putting aside for the first time in decades some long-standing family feud. Otherwise there was a single conversation that occasionally broke into laughter or lapsed into comfortable, reflective silence.

When Big Paeder walked in everyone's eyes fell on his

new boots, which were chestnut leather and the size of vegetable marrows.

'Size thirteen, said Big Paeder proudly. 'And I'll tell you another thing – mine is the biggest arm span in the county. Biggest span in the county. There's not a single man to beat it.'

Big Paeder must have been close to six-and-a-half feet, and although in his seventies, he was as strong as a wrestler. He was standing at the bar, too agitated to sit, and was twisting his cap back and forth as though he was wringing out a cloth. He looked around, half challenging, his blue eyes shining with fun.

Moments later he was leaning over the bar, his shoulders straining against the tweed of his jacket, his arms and huge hands splayed wide amongst the glasses of whiskey and stout, the empty bottles and packets of cigarettes and ashtrays. Someone found a tape-measure behind the bar and under the scrutiny of several witnesses placed one metal end under Big Paeder's longest finger. The tape was six foot long and when it was fully extended there was still some distance to Paeder's other hand. So the place where it ended was marked and the tape was extended again.

'Seven foot three inches!'

'Seven foot three inches!' said Big Paeder, straightening up, 'And there's not a man in the county to beat it.'

Several of the younger men tried, each gouging his

chin uncomfortably into the bar and stretching out his arms like a seal's flippers until his face turned red with the effort. Big Paeder didn't even supervise the measuring; he *knew* he had the biggest span in the county and with his back to the bar, his whiskey glass tilted precariously, he was busy talking about something else.

'Six foot.' The first candidate was hustled away.

'Six foot two.'

'Five foot eleven.'

'Biggest span in the county!' said Big Paeder when he was told the result. And as if to emphasise his superiority, he ordered a drink all round.

'Aye well,' said Connie Byrne who must have been about Paeder's age, 'He may have arms like a gorilla, but he's not the *broadest* man in the county.' He put his finger to his lips, mouthing 'shhhh', before adding with the very slightest of winks, 'Because *I* am.'

Some of the older men confirmed that Connie's chest was in fact three inches broader than Big Paeder's. Clearly they had compared measurements before, these men who had been to school together, worked in England, married, reared families together, and were now growing old together. But today Connie wasn't going to jeopardise his free drink. So when Big Paeder handed him his whiskey he merely thrust back his shoulders until his huge leather dispatch-rider's jacket strained across his chest, and said nothing.

Gradually the sky outside the window darkened as afternoon turned into evening. The curtains were drawn, fresh turf was stacked on the fire, damping its heat until bright flames burst through. Each time there was a lull in the conversation we could hear the wind as it howled through the village and whined in the telegraph wires. Sometimes our conversation would be stopped mid-sentence by the pelting of hail on the window or a gust of wind so violent I was convinced some damage must have been done and a loud crash would follow.

The talk turned to the weather again and to the terrible earthquake in India. Then three men who had spent most of the day in one of the pubs, either 'up above' or 'down below', remarked in slurred tones how strange it was they'd never been drunk. They'd enjoyed a drink all right, and they'd been tight and even stocious, but they'd never been drunk.

'There's only one way to tell when a man's drunk,' said Conal Byrne. 'And that's when he undoes the top button of his shirt to take a piss.'

By the time we left the pub, at around midnight, the Christmas lights had been put up in the village: red, green, blue and yellow bulbs strung between telegraph poles and the corners of buildings, zigzagging from one side of the main street to the other. And at either end of the street – by the telephone box outside Keany's and by

the single petrol pump – a Christmas tree was secured
in an oil drum filled with sand. The centre of the village
must have been relatively sheltered because the smell
of turf fires lingered in the air and the strings of lights
overhead merely swayed gently. But as we rounded the
corner past Gallagher's pub the full force of the Atlantic
wind was so strong we could hardly walk against it.

The Saturday night before Christmas all of the bars were
seething with noise and activity: in Keany's there was live
music; in O'Byrne's a darts match; in Gallagher's cards.
Unfamiliar faces in the pubs mixed with the regular ones.
Women who couldn't easily leave their children at night
had recruited a cousin or a neighbour to baby-sit and
were dressed to the nines for a rare night out with their
husbands. A lot of young people who had been working
abroad were home for the holidays. Everyone was pleased
to see them, clasping their hands warmly, buying them a
welcoming drink, enquiring how things were going over
the water.

Well after closing time the landlord of Gallagher's
began to gather the glasses and clear the tables. One final
cheer rose from the lounge as the last game of cards was
played and won and then gradually people started to leave.
It seemed that almost everyone who had played had won
a prize and, one after another, their faces flushed from
alcohol and the excitement of the game, they struggled

to negotiate the door while carrying one or even two cardboard boxes marked 'Turkey'.

But for many the night was young. There was a dance at the hotel a couple of miles away and all those who had cars or friends with cars piled in: all those who didn't hitched a lift or walked.

One evening, the sun came out for a moment and pools of blue appeared amongst the cloud. In the sunlight the grass on the hills was redder than copper, a sign of bad weather to come, and for a while, if you looked towards the horizon, you could watch each shower as it approached, a dark cloud trailing an undertow of white across the bay and then when it had passed, leaving a dusting of hailstones, the sun would come back and a row of rainbows appear far out over the sea.

On Christmas Eve the doors of the church were open for the carol service; light spilled out onto the windswept street. Cars drew up, their head- and tail- lights brokenly reflected in the wet. Doors were slammed and people hurried, grimacing, through the hostile night. In the shelter of the porch they smoothed their hair and clothes and greeted each other with rueful smiles and commiserations about the awful day. Then, composed, they went inside.

That night the church, which was usually stark and

bland, evoked something of the mystery so often lost from Christmas. The priest was wearing his yellow brocade cassock, the altar boys red and pristine white. Candles flickered on the altar and along the aisles, and at the front there was a candle-lit tableau of Mary and Joseph and the baby Jesus amongst stable animals and straw, and a Christmas tree decorated with balloons and a large sheet of paper on which the Ten Commandments had been copied in a child's painstaking hand.

The choir rose and the church filled with the sound of familiar carols. Wide-eyed children, wedged between their parents, stared about as if mesmerised by the candles and the music, half-dreaming in sleep-confused images of Santa Claus and his reindeer and three kings on camels making their way through the desert by the light of a star.

When the carols were over more people flocked in for Midnight Mass. Many had only reluctantly torn themselves from the pubs, knowing that if they missed Mass that night they'd have to get up early the following morning. One or two found a seat on the end of a pew, but most just gathered in the empty space at the back of the church.

Suddenly there was a commotion in the back rows. Colum MacGonagle had lost his cap and was standing up to check that he wasn't sitting on it, then bending down to make sure it hadn't fallen under his seat. His wife asked him if he'd definitely had it with him and he muttered impatiently that he wouldn't have left the house on a night like that without it. Their eyes started searching the rows of besuited men, their caps respectfully folded away in their pockets or on their laps. Feeling their gaze, people looked round enquiringly, then they too joined in the search.

A faint smell of whiskey drifted down from the back.

Then came the sound of deep relaxed breathing that was almost a snore.

Legally the pubs should have stayed closed on Christmas Day, but one or other of them always opened for a few hours at midday. So after Mass people hurried down through the wind and rain and, battered and dishevelled, ensconced themselves in the warmth, muttering despairingly that it would slice your ears off, or that it wasn't fit for a dog out there.

At the bar, Johnny and Ciaran, two fishermen who worked on the same boat, were sitting on high stools, and amidst the coming and going of people ordering drinks, the clatter and chinking of bottles and glasses, arguing. Johnny was complaining in tones that were both accusing and wounded that when he was coming to Mass that morning – all dressed up in his suit, wife and child waiting for him – he went to open his car door and this cat jumped out at him, scratching and spitting, and scaring him half to death.

Ciaran was silent. He had already told Johnny that the cat in his car had nothing to do with him.

'Honest to God, the stink of it. That cat must have spent the whole bloody night in there pissing itself.'

'I'm sorry, Johnny. Really, I'm sorry. But whoever put that cat in your car, it wasn't me.'

Johnny was unconvinced. One Christmas, a few years previously, Johnny had gone into his kitchen to have breakfast and found Ciaran's cat gorging itself on his turkey. Furious, he'd reached for his air gun and shot the cat just as it beat its retreat through the back door. Ciaran had never forgiven him. He said he'd loved that cat – Bubbles – with her snow-white fur and that little black patch on her chest.

'Jesus Christ, it could have given me a heart attack or something!'

'Johnny, I wish I *had* put that cat in your car. But unfortunately I didn't think of it.'

Still unconvinced, Johnny turned to Jack, another fisherman and the next most likely suspect. But Jack was busy telling someone about his trip to deliver the boat he'd been working on to its new owner in Chile.

'… and in the morning there'd be flying fish all over the deck and we'd fry them for breakfast. I had to work – a bit – because I was the cook, but the others just lay around all day, getting a sun tan and drinking Bacardi …'

The door opened and the sergeant walked in, telling us all politely but firmly that we had five minutes to drink up and leave the premises.

Later that day the power lines were brought down by the wind and the whole region lost its electricity. Maybe because it was Christmas, I couldn't help thinking of all the families in the village and the surrounding hills, sitting in the light of oil lamps or candles, with no television; maybe playing cards, eating and drinking. I also thought about all those people who were single, or childless, or whose loved ones for some reason couldn't come home, sitting by the light of the fire, staring into the flames.

On Saint Stephen's Day the traditional football match between improvised teams from two local villages had to be cancelled: not because of the cold or the wind and hail, which the players were used to, but because the field where they usually played – one of the few that was big enough and free of stones – was a foot deep in water. Everyone thought it would just be postponed for a day or two, but conditions never improved.

Day after day the storms continued. The sea was so dark it was almost black, or slate, or the uneven green of old glass bottles, and white where it smashed on the rocks, exploded in spray, and was swept, shimmering, over the cliffs.

One afternoon when I went for a walk along the beach I saw a couple of men in oilskins standing on the rocks at the far end, bracing themselves against the wind and hauling what looked like a rope out of the waves. They paused for a moment. One of the men seemed to be shouting to the other, but his words were lost in the wind. They took a few steps towards one another. The same man shouted again, and this time his companion shielded his ear with his hand, and nodded. The two of them leant back simultaneously, hauling again, and very slowly a net began to surface. Later I heard that the net had been washed up from a fishing boat that had gone down just a couple of weeks previously.

At the other end of the beach, in summer, a group of tourists had built a sculpture; a kind of totem pole based around a washed up log. They had decorated it with assorted beach debris: a pair of unmatched trainers, a desiccated John Dory, a battered and faded bleach container, a child's orange plastic sandal. Now all that remained was the fallen pole and a blue-and-white striped carrier bag, half-buried and too full of sand to do more than rustle slightly in the wind.

People said that sometimes during a storm you could walk along the beach and pick up grounded flat fish, if you could get there before the birds. And during the war the whole village used to rush down to the beach looking for ships' masts and beams which they'd sold for sixpence a foot for building, and everyone's eyes lit up as they remembered the crate-loads of biscuits that had been washed up, sealed and still fresh, and the vats of American moonshine as potent as local poteen.

But on that grey and blustery day there was nothing; just some strands of seaweed, the quivering ridges of foam left when the waves dropped back, and a few broken crab claws.

Most afternoons or evenings there was music in one or other of the pubs. Almost always it centred around Michael Boyle, the local fiddler, who people said was known throughout the world but still cut his own turf and kept sheep and cycled the five or so miles from his home into the village on an old and battered bicycle. In summer when he played he was billed in hotels and pubs as Michael Boyle and Friends, 'Friends' being whoever happened to join him. The day before New Year's Eve, in Keany's, his Friends consisted of: the priest who was alternating between tin whistle and flute – while his small dog Fifi bounced about on his lap – Bridget O'Maddigan with her guitar, and John Byrne also on fiddle.

When Mark and I arrived at about three in the afternoon, it was still too early to be really crowded; the atmosphere was intimate but lively. The players were sitting at the far end of a row of tables in the lounge while everyone else clustered around them. The tables were strewn with the usual collection of empty and full bottles and glasses, hats, gloves, cigarettes, lighters, rolling tobacco, pipes and ashtrays. A huge kettle was kept steaming on the range: it was the kind of day when people ordered hot whiskey and port.

For a while jigs and reels followed one another almost uninterrupted. Often the pace was so fast you wondered how the brain could compute the notes, the hands translate. In the past these same tunes had been played at weddings and ceilidhs and cross-road dances and still they evoked the cheerfulness of those occasions: the Wild Irishman, Gusty's Frolics, the Cuilin, The Cat that Kiddled in Johnny's Wig.

Everyone clapped, mesmerised, as Michael Boyle ended a complicated fiddle solo with an elaborate flourish.

'Can you play that one backwards, Michael?'

'That *was* backwards!'

For a while the players relaxed, talking, sipping their drinks, ordering more at the bar, and the sound of their music lapsed into the general drone of the pub. When she was ready to go on, Bridget O'Maddigan played on her own, and sang. Then a white-haired man launched into the Green Hills of Antrim, unaccompanied. When he had finished everyone turned to a young man, maybe in his mid-twenties, tall, with wavy black hair down to his shoulders and green eyes. He was someone I hadn't seen before and I wondered if he'd just come back for the holidays.

Slowly, he stood up and in a soft, clear voice started to sing. It was a ballad about a young man who had gone to England looking for work. He found it — hard work as a labourer, shovelling, swinging a pick, carrying hods. But all the time he was treated with taunts and suspicion born of the Troubles: Had he murdered someone? Did he make bombs in his bedroom? Eventually his drinking to enliven the nights took on a sinister turn. He ended up sleeping in a cardboard box in Piccadilly Circus and then, repeatedly in the refrain, lying under the neon lights, lonely, destitute, his heart aching for home, for his family, for Ireland. But he couldn't go back because he couldn't afford the flight.

For seconds after the man had sat down, pushing his long hair behind his ear and reaching for his drink, there was silence; as if everyone was privately dwelling on the fact that the man in the song could well have been their brother or uncle or son who disappeared to England and hadn't been heard of for so many years.

Three fishing boats went down off the west coast of Ireland over Christmas.

The skipper of one of them, the Amelis Delano,

described on the local news how, for hours, they had battled in force nine gales and waves that were over forty foot high. Then one thunderous wave had smashed a hole through the hull. Taking in water fast they maydayed another boat in the area, but conditions were so bad it couldn't get anywhere near them. Finally a wave crashed into the engine room, the engine failed and she ran aground. Only hours after the crew had been rescued, the boat was lost.

For their part, local fishermen worried that the bad weather wouldn't let up and there'd be no fishing for months on end, as had happened the previous year, when some of them had been living on benefits until well into March.

Because of the storms, too, the small boat which regularly made the eleven mile trip to Tory Island was unable to put out and the island was cut off for nearly two weeks. A helicopter went over once, with mail and bread and milk and a telephone engineer to repair the storm-damaged lines. But on several other occasions the helicopter, too, had been thwarted.

Even Aranmore Island, which was only just off the coast, was cut off for a day. There had been a picture in the paper of a group of men waiting to cross. Like most of the islanders, they had been in England working on motorways.

*

New Year's Eve was another big night out and then, a few days later, the television news showed scenes from airports around the country. All of them were crowded: mothers, fathers, uncles, aunts, grandparents saying goodbye and young people going. Some of them were glad to get away. But many more were in tears, either too distressed to face the camera, or openly and roundly haranguing the government for its refusal to create jobs, especially in the west, where the fate of entire communities often rested in their hands.

At midday in Keany's the fire had been lit but there was more smoke than flame and no warmth in it at all yet. Everything had been washed down and the floor, the bar, the tables and chairs were all still damp. There was a strong smell of bleach in the air.

Sitting on his regular stool at the edge of the bar, Paddy Gallagher was contemplating some money he had lost the day before. The money had been his own and his wife's English pensions. Bridget the barmaid was concerned and, trying to rekindle his memory, suggested two or three places he could have lost it or put it away and forgotten. She even offered to phone the Gardai and the priest in case someone had handed it in. But Paddy just said there was a picture of his brother in the wallet and if someone found it and wanted to give it back they could give it directly to him.

Outside, the Christmas tree by the telephone box had been blown down, oil drum and all, and was lying in a heap of dusty leaves and chocolate wrappers, its coloured lights still shining.

SMALLHOLDING

Sunlight slanted in brightly, mottling the patterned wall-paper, the dusty plates on the dresser. Michael poured boiling water into the tea-pot and set it down on the table. 'I'll fetch in the sheep the day,' he said. He'd waited almost a week for the rain to let up and the low water-logged clouds to lift from the mountain.

'Well, you've a good enough day for it,' Francie replied.

Michael took a packaged loaf from the bread bin, fetched the plates and cups and sat down with Francie. They poured their tea in silence, then stirred in milk and sugar.

'So you'll begin the clipping the morrow?' Francie asked.

'I will.'

When they'd finished eating, Francie reached for his leather jacket and went to the mirror to comb his hair. He said he was catching the bus to Donegal town; he needed a new string for his guitar.

Michael stood up and cleared away the plates.

'If you want,' said Francie, opening the door to go out, 'I'll give you a hand with the clipping the morrow.'

'Aye. Do that.'

When Francie was born, Michael had just turned twenty. Their mother, throughout Michael's boyhood, had passionately wanted another child. But year after year she remained barren. In the end she had seen it as 'God's will' and been almost content. She was shocked, therefore, to find herself pregnant. People had talked: especially as Francie grew into a quick-witted nimble child, whereas Michael and his father had both been solid, slow-moving. But she ignored the rumours. Without a doubt Francie's birth gave her life meaning.

It was soon after Francie was born that Michael had left for England.

On the mountain the wind rose suddenly, an unusual easterly wind, blowing out from the land, flattening the waves so the bay beneath was like beaten metal. In winter, old people said, this easterly wind carried colds and viruses. Michael leaned into it as he climbed, straining to keep his pace without falling back in the gusts. His eyes were smarting from the wind, dazzled by the brightness of the sun.

There were no fences on the mountain: all the village sheep were free to wander as they chose. But his own flock usually clung together, rarely straying from the grassy slope before the last steep climb to the top. This time, however, he couldn't see them. There were two of McGlinchey's ewes, marked with green on the shoulder and rump, but that was all. Michael pulled the binoculars out of his pocket and, bracing himself against the wind, adjusted the dial. Distant slopes, overblown and distorted, swam hazily into focus: sheep became stones, outcrops of rock turned into sheep. But none were his.

He cut in southwards, combing the hillside. The ground underfoot was sodden, not muddy, but saturated like a waterlogged sponge. Michael picked his way carefully, treading on stones and rushes and dry tussocks of heather, and avoiding the bog moss which occasionally floated like seaweed. Once again, he trained the binoculars and, this time, as he swung them around, he caught sight of his own sheep – one or two scattered ewes, then a group distinctively marked with the same faded red.

As he walked on, he noticed a pair of ravens spiralling in the white light of the sun. He followed their focus down to a dead ewe. She was sprawled on the bank of a stream: two hooves, a black speckled foreleg and a pair of horns emerging from a tangled heap of fleece. When he was closer he saw that she was one of his and that her flank still pumped gently. He bent over, trying to find out what was wrong. She flinched when he touched her, and scrabbled with her forelegs, attempting to stand. As he ran his hand down her back he noticed that her hind-quarters didn't move and that one back leg was severed and bleeding with two clear tooth marks in the thigh. A dog or perhaps a fox. He had a knife in his pocket and wondered whether to kill her; but he knew in his heart he couldn't do it. The ravens could finish her off or maybe he and Francie would come back later and carry her down to the track. He looked around for her lamb and found it a few yards away – all that remained was a cluster of stripped bones and a few flecks of fur.

There were many times when Michael wished that he had a dog. His father's Rex had died three years previously. After that Michael hadn't bothered with another one. Rex had been good with sheep, one of the best dogs in the parish, but most of them, however well you trained them, meant only one thing – trouble. Slowly he crossed the hillside, skirting the farthest ewes, then cutting in behind to chase them down towards the flock. The two ewes looked up when they saw him, grabbed a last mouthful of grass and, still chewing, trotted away into the hills, their lambs running behind. 'Ah you bastards,' Michael cursed.

By the time he had rounded up those two, another pair had fled but eventually he brought them all together. They were easier to manage when they started moving down the hill; instinctively, they clung together in a flock. Occasionally one would straggle, tempted in passing by a patch of grass; or a wayward group, for no apparent reason, would sheer off into the hills and he'd have to run after them and head them back, clapping his hands and shouting. But most of the time, if he moved steadily, driving but not frightening them, and occasionally skirting behind the flock, they stayed in line.

Slowly clouds spread back over the sky. At first they were distant, an elliptical haze that grew until dark shadows blotted out the sun. Michael looked down at the sea. It was grey now, with patches of aquamarine, but still flat, with seagulls bobbing over the waves. He passed the niche in the cliffs where in Garda raids they had once hidden poteen: and the place he had loved as a child where you looked down over the glen to see the whole farm laid out before you: the old house he now used as a byre, the new one behind it, the hayricks and turf pile, the row of pine trees that his father had planted for shelter, and the bottom meadow that his father had painstakingly claimed from the bog.

The lambs, Michael noticed, were doing well on the mountain grass. At three months old most of them were strong and sturdy, grazing one minute, then battering their mothers' teats as expertly as a baker's hands pummel dough.

By the time he reached the gentler slopes at the foot of the mountain, the cover of cloud was almost complete, obliterating the sun and the last pale traces of blue. It started to rain, just as it had for the past week: silent rain, soft and persistent.

Michael drove the sheep towards the stream, waited for the first few to reach the other side, and crossed over himself, balancing on slippery boulders and scrambling up the opposite bank. Then he joined the road. For a while there was no other traffic, but then a red Ford with Dublin number-plates careered round the bend. The driver saw the sheep and braked. The sheep stood stock still, dazed, then one at a time, they hurtled past the car and away off into the distance. Michael nodded in greeting to the driver, too proud to show his contempt.

Several hours later the sheep were safely in the bottom field, with the gate closed behind them.

Francie didn't come home that night. He had probably been to a disco in Donegal town and stayed over with a friend. Michael boiled a large pan of potatoes, fried some sausages and washed his meal down with tea. Then he switched on the television.

When Michael and Francie's father developed cancer, ten years previously, he was only fifty-five. Their mother, when she heard the diagnosis, had been beside herself with grief. She had always put her faith in God, and during the first months of his illness, she started going to Mass twice a day. She had even been on pilgrimages: once, with him, to the shrine at Knock where two young girls had seen the Virgin Mary and more recently a long-term paraplegic had risen up and walked; then on her own, to Lough Dearg for three grim days' penance; and finally to County Mayo, where on the last Sunday in July, she joined the dawn crowds and climbed Croagh Patrick, barefoot, in the rain. But there had been no miracle cure. After seven months' illness their father died. Michael had been in England at the time with a good job at a builders' yard in Haringey. But, dutifully, he had come home: to the farm and his mother and to Francie, who was still only a child.

The following morning, as soon as he had eaten, Michael went out to the field. The sheep were in a troublesome mood, but eventually, two at a time, they went barging into the byre. In the far corner they turned and stood huddled together, panting, their eyes wide with anticipation. Michael followed them in and, quickly, expecting a dash past his legs, he closed and bolted the door. In the gloom of the lichen-tinted window he could see almost nothing, but gradually his eyesight adapted. The sheep had begun to relax, nosing about in the straw. Michael moved a couple of buckets out of the way, then shifted the wooden bedstead he used as a door into the adjoining shed.

Going through, Michael rummaged around on the table – amidst the sheep dip and sheep mark, the antibiotics and bluestone, the bags and bins of fertilizer, ewe nuts and bran – and eventually located his hand-shears. Then, for a moment, he cast his eye over the sheep, wondering where to begin. Having singled one out, he moved quickly, lunging towards her. The ewe barged clumsily in through the flock. Michael grabbed hold of her horns and, bracing himself, pulled her up in her tracks. The ewe ducked her head lamely and Michael dragged her away from the flock and into the adjoining shed.

The ewe bleated hollowly and from the far side of the partition her lamb responded. Standing behind her, holding her forelegs, Michael tilted her on to her hind-quarters. Then, gripping her with his knees, he snipped a few tufts from her chest. The new growth, close to the body – as soft as a child's cuddly toy – was an inch long. She was definitely ready for shearing. Michael pulled her back further, grappling as she fought against him, and tumbled her onto her back. Immobilised, her legs in the air, she looked almost obscene with her balloon of a belly, her udder swollen with milk. Without releasing her head, Michael reached for a rope from the table and, rolling her over, tied three of her legs together as she struggled and thrashed.

He clipped her ribcage first, sweeping the dome of her belly from shoulder to rump in stripes towards her spine. Then he hauled her up by the horn, clipping across her back, and toppled her onto the opposite flank.

The contents of her stomach churned and resettled. She bleated, dropping the pitch to a drawn out groan. Michael moved to her hindquarters, carefully clipping the soft folds of flesh that surrounded her udder, her vulva and anus. The tail too was easy to nick – a sliver of skin that had to be stripped close because maggots bred in the soiled wool round it and from there could spread to the body. That was the part he had hated the most as a child when his father had first allowed him to help. Finally, he clipped her neck and pulled the whole fleece off, like a jumper, over her head.

When he untied the rope the ewe staggered to her feet and shook herself like a dog. She looked diminished: her fleece coarse and jagged and striped with blood where the shears had cut too close; her belly disproportionate to spindly legs and neck no broader than your wrist. When Michael pushed aside the door, she trotted through and her lamb, bleating in recognition, head-butted her newly-exposed, bulging teats.

Soon after midday there was a knock on the door. Michael left the ewe he was clipping to go and unbolt it. It was Francie. He was still wearing his good jeans and jumper and Michael gave him the old overalls that he kept on a hook by the door and a pair of half-mildewed leather boots.

All through the afternoon the two of them worked. Francie didn't have Michael's experience; he was slow, shearing only one fleece for Michael's two. But it was good to have help and, although they didn't talk much, there was companionship in simply being together and sharing the day. Sometimes when Francie wasn't sure what to do next he would stop, looking for Michael's advice, and the two of them would bend down over the one sheep. 'She's not ready for it yet,' Michael decided when Francie showed him a ewe with so little of the tight felt-like new growth that, if he had attempted to clip her, the loose older wool would have fallen apart like hand-fuls of hair. 'We'll try her again in a month.' So Francie released the ewe and sent her totting back, undisfigured. Another time when Francie had trouble inserting the shears between the straggle of old wool and the hide, Michael agreed, 'It's tight on her.' Then, checking again, 'Ah, sure go ahead anyway.'

But it wasn't just the clipping; there were any number of other jobs to be done. The sheep's hooves had to be pared. One ewe, which Michael had noticed on the mountain, was limping badly and when he picked up her foot to look at it, it was swollen and putrid, so he cut out the badness with a sharp knife until it dripped blood onto the straw, then soaked it in a plastic container of copper-sulphate solution. There were lambs with pulpy kidney, too, and lung worm and a ewe with mastitis so bad that one of her teats was as hard as a football. Michael injected her with antibiotics.

'If she gives birth to twins next year,' he said to Francie, 'One of them will die.'

When Michael had come back from England, he knew nothing at all about sheep. Occasionally when he was a boy his father had asked him to help: it had been his job, for example, when the sheep were coming in to block off the road on the far side of the gate, waving his arms and shouting, so the flock veered off and went thundering into the field; and in spring there'd been orphaned lambs to be raised by the hearth. In England he'd forgotten the skills that he'd learned: only sensations remained in his mind – the sound of the sheep's hooves clattering over concrete; their tight curls and surprisingly hard little lips mouthing his hand. But, with a flock of his own, he had gradually learned. He had talked to other sheep farmers, he had watched and he had listened, too proud to ask for advice. His father, they said, had a way about him with sheep, instinctively knowing which of the ewe lambs to keep in each new crop, which ones to sell; which would be good breeders; which, when they got older to put with each of his rams, the pure Scottish Black Face or the cross-bred Leicester. In those days there had been money in sheep. The wool had been exported to Britain and to China and Russia. There had been a thriving tweed industry at home. But all that had changed.

*

Michael finished another ewe, rolled up the fleece with the loose tail- and chest-clippings wrapped inside, and tossed it onto the pile.

That night Francie didn't go out. It was late when they left the byre and they were tired. Michael heated a can of beef stew for them both and fried some leftover potatoes and they drank milk with it, followed by tea. Afterwards they watched a comedy show on the television and laughed together even when it was over.

For exactly one month after their father died, their mother had mourned with a suffering barely endurable, even to watch. Then, quite suddenly, she put it behind her, devoting herself to her sons: to Michael, the breadwinner; and to Francie, whom she had wanted to stay on at school and try for a college place in Dublin. In the morning when the two of them got up there was always a fire in the grate and a warming meal on the table: porridge or bacon and eggs and home-made brown bread. Then in the evening they would be welcomed back with the signs of her work: a warm clean house, a pile of neatly-folded ironing, some freshly-baked cakes or scones on the rack by the range.

The summer was always the busiest time. When Michael had finished the clipping and before he took the ewes back to the mountain, there was dipping to do, and dosing, inoculating, re-marking and then the wether lambs to be rounded up and sold to a dealer. That year's prices were low. Everyone was despondent. Some of the farmers were holding back, waiting to auction their lambs at the end of the season, assuming that prices would rise. Others feared the opposite. As well as the work with the sheep, there was turf to be cut and saved and hay to be harvested, baled and brought home.

Sometimes, before he went to bed, Michael would go outside for a last look at the day's work. There was satisfaction in the warm smell of cut hay and the fields' changing contours during the harvest. Once when he went out at two in the morning, there was still light in the sky and in the distance towards the town, he could see a glimmering trail of car headlights. The hotel bar would probably still be open, crowded with tourists and migrants home for the summer. There would be music and laughter and afterwards maybe a dance. Then, when everything had closed, couples would make their way blearily home as dawn broke over the hills.

Francie almost never came home. As the long days merged into weeks then months, Michael knew he was seeing a woman. Without anyone telling him he also knew who she was – the red-haired Dublin artist who was renting the holiday cottage down by the strand.

Autumn came and with it a chill in the air. The potato patch that in summer looked, from a distance, like a green carpet laid out in front of the house, was now brown and bare with only the withered stalks jutting out of the earth. Michael fetched in the sheep. On the mountain the north-easterly wind in his face was as sharp as a whiplash. It smelled of winter. For almost a week he dipped and dosed; he docked the lambs' tails and sheared the ewes' rumps – 'taking off their knickers,' as his father had said – ready for the ram when they came on heat. Then he loaded the ewe-lambs onto the trailer to take them down to the mart. It was the last auction of the year and Michael was hoping that prices had risen. They hadn't. The auctioneer's hammer fell on his lambs at a pitiful price.

One morning he awoke to the sudden awareness that that day was the day of the Ram Fair. On impulse he decided to go. When he was a boy he had loved taking the sheep to the fairs with his father. There used to be one almost every month throughout the summer, each in a different part of the county, and you could buy and sell wether lambs at one, ewes at another, cattle somewhere else. But the Ram Fair was always the best. Everyone went.

It was a wet day. Fine rain hung in the air, barely falling, and a bank of cloud blotted out the hills. Michael left the old Cortina parked amongst other cars and trailers on the side of the road and walked down to the town. It was a broad street, designed for fairs and at one time its entire width used to be blocked off with crowds of people and flocks of sheep jostling each other as they barged their way up and down. Now it was almost empty, just a broad expanse of wet tarmac with runnels of water trickling into potholes and gutters. Three or four ewes were tethered to the railings outside one of the houses and a group of men had gathered round the open ramp of a trailer, peering inside. There were market stalls in the open space beside the church: one selling china and crockery, another with gumboots and waterproof jackets, and one selling jeans and T-shirts and fashionable dresses.

Michael rarely drank but because it was fair day he allowed himself a whiskey. The bar was busy, but quieter than it often was on a Saturday night or a Sunday morning after Mass. Michael ordered a Powers and greeted the few people he knew.

'It's quiet enough,' one of them commented.

'Aye, but it's early yet.'

Michael poured himself a bottle of stout. The pub was being renovated, extended for the summer influx of tourists, and from time to time the wave of voices was broken by hammering in the back room or the whirr of an electric drill.

Michael ordered another Powers.

When he went outside again, warmed by the alcohol, he half-expected the noise and the bustling crowds of the old fairs, the excitement in the air and the strong smell of sheep. There were a few more people: women and children, wrapped in waterproofs, surveying the market stalls; farmers, almost all of them old, buying and selling, haggling over prices. And there were more sheep, tethered to lamp-posts and railings and the tow-bars of trailers. But little had changed, only the rain which was teeming down more heavily than before.

At the end of October, Michael went to the byre to fetch out the ram. He had kept him inside for over a week, feeding him, building his strength. Now he looked in his prime. Michael was proud of his ram – a pure-bred Black Face, heavy, with well-set hindquarters and magnificent horns framing his 'blown' nose and shrewd eyes. When Michael released him, he threw back his head, curling his lips, his nostrils flared to the scent of the ewes. Then he trotted away down through the field, his long fleece sweeping his ribs like curtains. He investigated one ewe after another and, when he found one that had come on heat, he batted her flank, first gently with one of his horns, then with his foreleg. Finally he mounted her.

That winter seemed especially hard. Gales came lashing in from the sea, pelting the house with downpours of hailstones. Once, in the night, Michael awoke to the sound of roof-tiles clattering down to the ground. The following day he weighted the edge of the roof with sand-bags and stones tied down with rope. Soon afterwards he was woken again by the black plastic sheeting that covered the bales in front of the house flapping as it ripped and worked itself free.

At Christmas Michael was invited to the holiday cottage down by the strand. He didn't go, but he often thought about Francie and the Dublin artist. He pictured them in the evening going down to the pub and, at night, warm in their big double bed. They said in the town she was only here for a year. Michael hoped it was true.

When Michael and Francie's mother died, two years previously, Francie had just passed his exams. He had intended to apply to college but his mother's ambition for him had been his incentive, and after she died, he hadn't even filled in the forms. Her death, at fifty-eight, came as a shock. One morning she had made them both breakfast as usual, and in the evening, when Michael came up from the byre, she had been dead. For two days the brothers watched over her body, greeting friends and neighbours who had come to the wake. Everyone mentioned her kindness, her sense of fun. They also said that her dead face looked calm.

January and February seemed interminable. For a week Michael went up to the top field to remove stones, so that in summer the hay could be cut with a tractor. Some of the stones were so big that without help he couldn't begin to extract them. There were other jobs to be done as well: the potato patch to be dug ready for planting; the rushes in the bottom field to be sprayed and uprooted; the byre roof was leaking and the fence alongside the road was so rickety you could have pushed it down with your hand. But nothing got done. Every evening, just before nightfall, he fed the sheep. Wrapped in an oilskin jacket and gumboots, he trudged back and forth through the mud carrying armloads of hay and buckets of ewe nuts to the racks and troughs and the stampede of welcoming sheep. Otherwise he didn't go out, didn't work in the fields, didn't go to Mass any more, never went to the pub. Sometimes he wondered if it was worth his while even feeding the sheep. The lambs would be bigger than if the pregnant ewes had been eating only grass, and more would survive. But what did it matter? There was no money in wool and the market for meat was flooded with cheap lamb from abroad.

Week after week Michael stared out the window, watching the changing greys of the sky: the high formless grey that blotted out colour on bland indeterminate days; the leaden storm clouds rolling in from the sea; the fog that clung to the fields obscuring the sheep and the wind-buckled sally trees that bordered the stream.

March came. When Michael went outside to refill the turf bucket from the pile by the byre, the sun felt warm through an ice-cold wind. The first lambs were born, strong and healthy. By Saint Patrick's Day there were six, three pairs of twins. One morning Michael came in from the field exhausted but gratified. He had been up for most of the night helping a ewe with a difficult birth. He was surprised to see Francie sitting at the kitchen table, drinking tea. Michael took off his boots and washed his hands. Then Francie told him he was moving to Dublin: Dympna's new job teaching evening classes at art school started in April and he himself had a place at the college.

A JOB ON THE BOATS

'I remember there was one young buck mad keen for a job on the boats. He'd pestered the skipper for over a year and in the end he was given a start. When he turned up at the quay he was as happy as a kid at Christmas. Everything was fine for a while. He was sitting in the galley with the rest of us, drinking tea and having the crack, but as time went by he grew quieter and quieter and suddenly he leapt to his feet and rushed to the stern. He near turned himself inside out that night, and for the rest of the trip he didn't once rise from his bunk, just lay there, his head in the sleeping bag, groaning. When we got in, ten days later, he was so weak he had to be helped off the boat. He went straight to his car, started her up, and that was the last we saw of him.'

Patrick was the first deep-sea fisherman I had met. It was in the pub at the end of summer, September, I think, and early evening. There were five or six of us there at the time: one conversation.

'Sometimes,' said Joseph, the barman, 'When you're out in a boat you feel so ill you just wish it would sink and that was the end of it.'

'Even the ferry to Wales can be bad enough at times.'

'Aye, but at least you're back on the land in three or four hours. It's different when you know you'll be out there for days: you panic, your heart starts pounding and you're sweating away like a pig. It's not just the motion of the boat, it's the smell that gets to you – the mixture of rotten fish and bilge and engine oil.'

'Do you still get sick?'

'Oh aye. If it's a bad day and the boat's been tied up for a couple of weeks, you have to get used to the rock 'n' roll.'

'I'd die if my life depended on fishing. It makes me sick just watching the boats from the pier.'

'The trick is to eat. I know when you're sick the last thing you feel like is food, but there's nothing worse than to be roaring away with only your guts to bring up. If someone gets sick on the boat, I'd give him porridge or a tin of peaches or pears, to settle the stomach. If you can face it, a bowl of whiting soup first thing in the morning's good, because it brings up the wind. But the one way you're guaranteed to get sick is to go out on a dirty night with a bellyful of beer or a hangover.'

Over the months Mark and I came to know Patrick better. Often when he was back for a few days between trips or when the weather was too rough to go out he'd talk to us about fishing: about his boat, the Mary Louise, a ninety-foot wooden-hulled trawler; about the crew and other Killybegs fishermen; about the ups and downs of the white fishing industry. He was a good storyteller, and one day, when we were feeling adventurous, we asked if there was any chance of them taking us with them. Patrick looked surprised, then said as far as he was concerned there'd be no problem, although we'd need to talk to the skipper.

But the skipper's mind was made up: the boat was no place for a woman. Maybe one day if they went out on a short trip he'd consider it. At the moment it was ten days at a time: the weather could change in a flash and if I got sick or scared there'd be no turning back. It wasn't the kind of life a woman could stand, but if Mark wanted to go he'd be welcome.

The day that Mark was due to go out, a gale was blowing; the waves in the bay were as high as I had seen them and the beach was a quivering mass of foam. Patrick assured us that it would be a good few days before it settled. So Mark went to the pub that night, celebrating his reprieve. But early the following morning there was a knock at the door. It was Patrick. He had just had a call from the skipper: they were to be at the boat in a couple of hours. We looked out of the window. The sea was almost as angry as the day before, the waves smashing themselves furiously over the rocks. We thought Patrick was joking, but he shrugged. Mark turned white – then groaned and said he had a hangover.

By the time Patrick came back for him, in just over an hour, Mark was feeling better. He had had something to eat and packed a bag with the few things he would need: a sleeping bag and pillow, a change of clothes, a towel, a wash-bag and his camera. He reached for his yellow oilskins from the hook by the door, put on his wellingtons and the two of them set off in Patrick's car.

For the next few days I thought about Mark almost constantly. In the mornings when I woke the first thing I did was to look at the sea, and every evening I tuned into the shipping forecast on the radio. The wind had dropped almost completely the first night they were out, as Patrick predicted it would, and for a day or two after-wards conditions seemed to be good. I stopped worrying. The wind became light to moderate, gusting force four or five, and dropped again. Then on the seventh day I switched on the radio as usual: 'Attention all shipping in the meteorological regions Rockall and Malin, the following gale warning has been issued...'

I decided to go and see Annie, Patrick's wife. She was welcoming as always and invited me in for a cup of tea. I played with the baby for a few minutes while she was boiling the kettle and filling the cups. The three older children were sitting on the sofa with one of their cousins, watching television. When Annie came in with the tea she gave them some money and told them to go down to the shop for a packet of biscuits.

'Did you hear the forecast?' I asked her as she sat down.

'Aye, they're giving out for gales.'

'What do you think they'll do?'

'Well,' she said, 'They could decide to come back, or they could put into the nearest harbour. It all depends where they are. If they're miles from anywhere, they might just batten down the hatches and wait for it to pass.'

'Do *you* worry?' I asked her.

'Not so much now. I used to when he first went out. But then again, at that time, with the first wee one on the way, I was just glad that he had the job.'

The children burst in with the biscuits. Annie opened the packet, offered me one, took one herself and handed the packet back to the children.

'Any other time,' she said, 'he'd ring when he got back in so I could go and pick him up. He usually takes the car to the harbour and leaves the keys in one of the bars so I can collect it. But these last few days I haven't had the chance, so he'll be able to drive.'

'Oh well, I expect we'll hear from them soon enough.' Just talking to her had reassured me. 'If you need the car you could come with me tomorrow. I have some shopping to do in any case.'

All through the night the wind whistled round the

house. Sometimes the gusts were so strong I thought that a window would break or a sheet of asbestos would be lifted clean off the roof. In the morning, restless from tossing and turning, I was glad to get up and drive over to Annie's, as we'd arranged. She'd left the baby with a neighbour and the three older children were at school, so it was just the two of us as we set off in the car.

'It must have been bad over here in the night,' I said, watching the spray blowing up over the cliffs. Her house was close to the open sea, unlike mine in the relative shelter of the bay.

'Aye, it was bad enough.'

'I tried to light a fire this morning, but the room just filled with smoke.'

'I'd say they'll probably come back in. The forecast's giving out for worse gales today.'

When we arrived in Killybegs I parked the car and we walked down to the pier, just in case they were there. A lot of boats had come in from the storm, but we couldn't recognise them because the tide was low and all we could see from that distance were the masts and derricks, two or three abreast alongside the pier. A couple of container lorries were parked by the corrugated iron auction shed, and fork lift trucks were beetling around unloading boxes of mackerel and herring from the boats.

As we reached the edge of the pier and looked down, the first boat we saw was the Mary Louise. Patrick and Mark and one or two others, wearing oilskins and wellies, were sluicing the deck with brooms and a hose, and stacking up fish boxes. Patrick saw us almost immediately and came up to the wheelhouse, which was about the same level as the pier. He opened the window and shouted across that the fishing was poor and then, with a wink, that Mark was a Jonah. Not only that – he was the only one who hadn't been sick. Although he was shouting it was hard to hear what he was saying over the wind and the noise of the engine, so we arranged to meet in the Anchor Bar in a couple of hours, after they had finished their work and we had done our shopping.

When they came into the bar Mark especially looked windblown and happy.

'How did you know we were in?' said Patrick.

'We didn't. We just came for the car.'

Patrick looked suspicious but it wasn't until much later, when I met Johnny, another fisherman, that I understood why.

'All skippers have access to ship-to-shore phones,' he explained, 'so their families can always find out where they are. But no fisherman likes to be worried about, so the last thing they want is their wives and girlfriends ringing up, making enquiries.'

He laughed. 'But the best way to embarrass a fisherman – if you really want to cause trouble – is to write to him on the boat. I know because it happened to me a

couple years back when we were fishing out of Howth for
six months. One day this pink envelope arrives: Johnny
Mulhern, The Orion, care of The Harbour Master ...'

That evening, when we were back at home, Mark told me
about the trip.

They didn't go out for a long time after they left the
house that morning – they were busy preparing equipment and loading ice into the hold – and then when
they'd finished that they went to the Anchor for some fish
and chips and a drink or two. By then, he said, he was no
longer nervous, he'd developed a resigned, come-what-
may attitude and was even looking forward to it.

He and Patrick were the first to go on watch so they
settled themselves in the wheelhouse and as the boat left
the harbour and set sail in the open sea, Patrick showed
him the equipment and explained how it all worked.
Mark said it made you wonder how they managed before
computers, when there were no navigation plotters and
no echo sounders to tell you where the fish were.

For the three hours they were on watch they had to
make sure that no boat approached too close on the radar
and that the automatic pilot stayed on course. Every five
minutes a buzzer sounded and if for any reason they hadn't
cancelled it within a couple of seconds an ear-piercing
alarm would have gone off right through the boat until
someone came to investigate.

It took thirty-one hours to steam to Rockall, where they fished. During that time there was nothing to do, so when they weren't on watch they slept, played cards, watched videos, ate, slept again. It was good to sleep as much as possible because when they reached the fishing grounds the nets were shot every five hours, and in between the fish had to be sorted, gutted, stored away, and the nets cleaned and sometimes repaired.

The first time they hauled it was the middle of the night. There was no shelter deck on the boat, so they worked in the open air in the bright light of the arc lamps. The fish were spilled onto the fore deck where they had to be sorted into boxes according to type and size. There were plaice, sole, haddock, halibut, hake, pollack and 'junk fish' – conger eels, gurnards, jellyfish – which they threw back into the sea. Then when all the fish were sorted they had to be gutted and cleaned – the big ones by hand, the small ones mechanically – and packed into boxes of ice in the hold.

Mark said that when the weather was rough the work was doubly difficult, certainly for him and for the first few days until he was used to the motion. Most of the time the boat was broadside to the swell, and as it rolled, unless you were holding on to something, you'd be thrown from one side of the deck to the other along with the fish you were sorting. Sometimes, he said, if you looked over the edge you were convinced that an on-coming wave would swamp the down-tilt of the deck, and then at the last minute it would curl away under the hull as the boat lurched back in the other direction. And if you'd looked over the opposite edge at the same time, you'd have seen the sea falling away beneath you in a dizzying thirty foot drop. But occasionally the rhythm of the boat would be out and a wave would come smashing over the deck. Once when this happened Mark looked up and noticed that Patrick, who had been standing at the stern, had disappeared in a great deluge of spray. He was horrified, convinced Patrick must have been swept overboard. But moments later as the water subsided he saw him again, scrambling to his feet, drenched but grinning.

Meal times – for those who could face them – were the high points of the day with everyone sitting round the big table in the galley while George the chef served bacon, egg, sausage and beans for breakfast and maybe roast beef or chicken, fresh fish or lamb followed by dessert for dinner, and tea. No expense was spared and George was a good chef. Apparently he made expert meals on shore as well as at sea and if he had one complaint about cooking at sea it wasn't the lack of fresh ingredients or the difficulty of balancing pans on the stove in a storm, but the fact that although the crew appreciated his cooking, they allowed him no scope for experiment. Each time he served up something unfamiliar such as moussaka, cassoulet or even curry, however impressed he was with the results, they would complain.

George had been working on the boats for over ten years. Originally he came from Dublin and from there he went to England where he spent three years studying at Cambridge. No one seemed to know how from there he had ended up on the west coast, fishing. Rumour had it he was writing a book about the boats, but when Mark mentioned it he laughed. On shore he drove a sports car and was known for his snappy dressing, not only on special occasions, but often just walking around town or drinking in one of the pubs. On the boat he was like a mother, making sure that everyone, especially new members of the crew, felt comfortable and at home.

Mark said it wasn't just George and Patrick who looked after him: the entire crew was welcoming and friendly. Even when they were busy on deck someone would take time to explain what was happening and to show him how he could help, or at least not get in the way. On several occasions when they were shooting the nets Patrick had reached for him and hauled him clear of the chains as they unfurled down the side of the boat releasing the great trawler doors to the bottom of the sea.

'They did call me a Jonah, though,' he said.

'What did they mean by that?'

'I suppose that I brought them bad luck. The fishing was the worst it's been all year. They only caught a hundred and nineteen boxes, and usually it's over two. That means, when you add up the cost of diesel, ice, insurance and all the other overheads, they made an overall loss. And that has to come out of the next trip's profits before they even begin to be paid.'

'Were you at Rockall all the time?'

'No just four or five days. There were hardly any fish there – one or two of the nets came up with nothing but jellyfish – so the skipper decided we'd move on towards Tory Island. Then it started to get rough and the nets were being snagged and torn – one night we were up until dawn repairing equipment. So when we heard the gale warning the skipper decided there was no point in carrying on.'

'And did you really not get seasick?'

'I felt a bit queasy at times – but I wasn't going to let on.'

I had almost resigned myself to not going out on a trawler when I met Johnny and Ciaran, two young fishermen who worked on the same boat, the Orion, fishing herring, pair-trawling with another boat, the Antoinette, usually off the south west coast on trips that were rarely more than two or three days at a time.

When I explained that I'd been trying to go out on a boat, Johnny said: 'Jesus, you'd be more than welcome with us. You'd be best off on a short trip like that – at least if you do get sick you won't have to suffer long. You'll have to talk to the boss of course, but I can't see that he'll mind.'

When Mark and I drove to the skipper's house there was snow on the ground. His wife and daughter were putting up Christmas decorations, standing on chairs and laughingly considering whether sticky tape or drawing pins would be less damaging to the paintwork. A warm smell of Sunday dinner filtered through from the kitchen. We sat down with a cup of coffee and the skipper told us about the herring industry and the unpredictability of catches and prices from one year to the next. Johnny was right: we'd be welcome on board any time.

The night we were due to go out we had arranged to meet Johnny and Ciaran in the pub an hour or so before closing time. It was Saturday night and the bar was crowded. Judging by the empty glasses on the table in front of them Johnny and Ciaran had been there for some time. When he saw us come in Johnny stood up and asked us what we wanted to drink. Remembering Patrick's advice I asked for a Coke, but Johnny bought me a double brandy, insisting that it was worse to be stone cold sober your first time out than it was to be drunk.

'Did you hear the forecast?' said Ciaran, taking a sip from the Guinness that Johnny had brought him. 'They're giving out for gales tomorrow. Force eight and nine. Nor-westerly.'

'I didn't hear that.' I had listened to the forecast earlier and been relieved that the cold still weather of the last few days was supposed to continue.

'Ah, the television and radio would have missed it. This was on the satellite forecast.'

'Are you serious?' I turned to Johnny for confirmation.

'I'd say we'll be feeding the seagulls tomorrow.'

The boat was due to go out at two, and at midnight, when the pub closed, the four of us set off in one car. The road was almost deserted, just three or four cars going back from the pubs or on to dances and parties. Killybegs too was quiet, apart from the bass drone of rock music coming from a disco somewhere. The Christmas lights were on in the main street and the lights on the boat, red and green indicating port and starboard, white on the mast and derricks, were reflected on the dark harbour water. It was a cold night, frosty again, and as calm as a baby's breathing.

We made our way down to the pier. The blue-and-white Orion and the red-and-white Antoinette, both stained with streaks of rust, were moored side by side amongst other boats. Their engines were running, ready to leave.

Johnny and Ciaran stepped on board and Mark followed. I looked down at the three-foot expanse of water between the boat and the pier, with swirls of pale scum floating on top and pieces of wood and seaweed and litter, and for a moment my courage failed. Johnny and

Ciaran had stepped easily on to the railing surrounding the boat and from there jumped down on to the deck. But you had to be confident, to trust your balance and not look down, not even think about slipping or how difficult it would be to surface if you sank down under the boat. I threw across my wellingtons and overnight bag and, not wanting to be in trouble before the trip even began, I braced myself and stepped across.

When we were all on board Johnny showed us around the boat: she was built in Holland in the mid-twenties, steel-hulled, ninety-foot long – the same size as the Mary Louise, though with her cover-deck she looked bigger. He showed us the fishing equipment: the hydraulic winch and the great drum with its coils of net, culminating in the 'money bag' where the fish collected; the net-sounder cable which ran alongside it registering the size of the catch on a gauge in the wheelhouse; the chutes down which the fish were channelled into three iced storage tanks. He found a couple of sets of sound mufflers and took us down to the engine room, warning us that the heat and the noise were unbearable. He showed us where the life jackets and inflatable rafts were stored. Most of the crew, he said, had taken a safety course, but lowering the rafts into the water the right way up was difficult enough in itself, let alone getting the crew on board when virtually none of them was able to swim.

'She's a great boat,' he said with affection. 'A bit top-heavy, though. Just a wee bit too rolly.'

We followed him down a ladder to the galley where Martin the chef was reading a week-old tomato-stained Irish Press that must have been there since the previous trip, and Ciaran was at the sink filling a battered-looking kettle. When it had boiled he made us all a cup of tea and opened a packet of biscuits and we sat on bench seats around the big table with its rubberised mesh cloth to stop things slipping off when the sea was rough, talking and laughing, still high from the alcohol. Gradually other members of the crew arrived and when Johnny or Ciaran introduced us most of them shook hands and said, 'You're welcome'; others just nodded, not knowing what to say. For a while everyone milled around the galley making cups of tea and coffee, opening and re-opening the fridge for butter and cheese, and the cupboards for jam and peanut butter and packets of biscuits and crisps. In time most of the crew went to bed leaving just the four of us still sitting around the table. At two o'clock a bell rang as the boat pulled out into the harbour and soon afterwards we too went to our bunks.

Leading the way downstairs Ciaran switched on the dim overhead light in the bunkhouse, and talking quietly, showed us where we were sleeping. The bunks were set into wooden panelling one on top of another on either side of the curved hull of the boat. Each was about three foot wide and deep enough to sit up in, with a raised board to stop you rolling out in high seas.

As I laid out my sleeping bag and climbed into bed I wondered whose bunk this was normally and whether he'd mind me using it. On the wooden shelf at the back there was a half-drunk bottle of Coke, two or three old disposable razors, a stack of empty cigarette packets and a toothbrush. Pinned to the wall was a photograph of three young boys, presumably his children.

For a long time I lay awake adjusting to the unfamiliar surroundings. The bunkhouse was below the water-line and it was hot and airless, and noisy with the clatter and rumble of the engine below. It wasn't a rough night. Occasionally the boat lurched and rolled as an exceptional wave churned through her path, but apart from that the only noticeable movement was the juddering engine. Every few hours the overhead light went on and I looked out from my bottom bunk by the door to see the dark legs and feet of someone coming back from his shift on watch. Wordlessly he woke up the next man and taking off his shoes, trousers and sweater, climbed into bed. Moments later a second pair of legs made its way out and when all was quiet the automatic light clicked and switched itself off.

I wondered how long it would take, how many trips, before the noises and comings and goings were as familiar as traffic sounds in the city and whether, in time, the motion of the boat would nurturingly rock you to sleep.

Once or twice I woke with a start as the boat tilted me helplessly down to the side of my bunk, dipping so low I was convinced she would keel over, before finally lurching back and falling away in the other direction. I felt the blood rush to my head, then drain away. My hands were sweating, my chest and stomach felt tight and constricted. I wondered if these were the early symptoms of seasickness, if it would be better – when the time came – to rush for the deck or the toilet and if I'd be able to find the light switch and the way up the steps. Then, with a groan, the boat settled to her previous rhythm and I drifted back to sleep.

I was finally deeply asleep when the bell rang again and I opened my eyes to see people struggling out of their sleeping bags, leaning over rummaging for socks and boots, putting them on. Johnny, on his way out past my bunk, stopped and told me they'd found a shoal of herring six miles away and everyone was getting ready. I glanced over at Mark in his bunk at the other side of the boat: he sat up in his sleeping bag, looked over to see if I was awake, and yawned.

In the galley the kettle was boiled and re-boiled as people made drinks and prepared bowls of cereal and slices of bread. I took my cup of tea away from the kitchen area, and sat at the table, not wanting to think about food or even talk to anyone. Ciaran was sitting quietly opposite

me, looking pale and hung-over and taking great gulps
from a large bottle of lemonade.

After I'd drunk the tea it was good to get outside into
the fresh air. It was just beginning to get light: a grey
drizzly day, disappointing after the sunshine and clarity
of the previous week. In the distance soft rainclouds hung
low over Killala bay and the coast of Mayo and for miles
around the sea was as grey and gently undulating as the
clouds.

'It's looking bad.' Johnny had come up behind me and
was following my glance. 'I'd say it's definitely brewing
up for a storm.'

'But it's as calm as anything out there.' I was convinced
by now that his 'storm' was a joke.

'Ah you'd have to know the sea to read the signs.'

Mark had also come out now and the two of us talked
for a while and then followed Johnny up the ladder into
the wheelhouse. The skipper was sitting at the control
chair behind an array of computers and navigation equipment. We hadn't seen him the night before as he had his
own private cabin adjoining the bridge, and he greeted us
and welcomed us on board.

Johnny showed us the echo sounder and pointed out
the shoal of herring, a red blob on the computer screen
amongst blue and yellow and grey stripes of interference.

'It works by sending sound waves to the bottom of the
sea. As the echo bounces back it shows types of fish in

different colours according to the density of the shoal and the depth. Herring are pink. Roe herring – which is what we're after – are dark red because they swim closer to the surface when they're spawning. Before people had all this, they just knew from experience where the fish would be and when they thought they were close, they shone a bright light into the water. The herring, frightened by the glare, flipped out of the water, giving themselves away by the white flash of their underbellies.'

As we talked the skipper was muttering under his breath and growing increasingly agitated. The boat was almost alongside the herring now, but we couldn't shoot the nets until the Antoinette joined us. Presumably the skipper could see her on the radar, but looking back the way we had come, across the mist and rain and the flat grey sea, there was no sign of her at all. For the third time since we had been in the wheelhouse the skipper picked up the phone and roared: 'Are you fucking rowing that boat or what?'

By the time the Antoinette did catch up the fish had disappeared, and cursing, the skipper wheeled the boat round trying to find them. She was broadside to the swell now and rolling in a steady rhythm that made my head feel light. When we eventually found the fish, Johnny rushed out on deck where the rest of the crew were waiting.

The sound of the engine dropped to a drone and the boat slowed down, almost stopping. The Antoinette drew up beside her, edging so close we could see the individual features of the crew – a black moustache, a ginger beard, creased blue eyes – under the peaked hoods of their oilskins. When she was as close as she could safely be, Johnny threw across a buoy on a coiled rope attached to the net. One of the crew lunged for it but it fell short, landing in the water. Johnny reeled it in and threw again. This time they caught the rope and attached it to their winch.

The boats pulled apart, picking up speed, and the net splayed out between them. I was still in the wheelhouse, watching through the open window, not wanting to get in the way of the ropes and hawsers and the crew as they worked. I thought about Johnny and Ciaran rocking with laughter as they told me how one day the skipper had leaned out of this same window while they were working in a force eight gale and, from the comfort of the wheelhouse, yelled, 'Call yourselves fishermen? Yous'd make fishermen *cry*'.

But today he left them in peace, looking out only occasionally, saying nothing. Every so often, as we were trawling, one of the crew would come up to the wheelhouse to find out how we were doing. The net sounder recorded the weight of the catch on the screen: thirty tons, thirty five tons, forty tons and still going up. Everyone was exhilarated watching the dial shift further and further as the fish poured in. Johnny came in, high on adrenalin. 'That's Christmas taken care of,' he said. 'Now for the beer!'

Eventually the dial quivered, almost coming to rest as the flood of fish slowed to a trickle, and at a word from the skipper Johnny and the others went back on deck.

Slowly the net was winched in and coiled round the big drum at the stern. Finally, the 'money bag' rose to the surface, an enclosed mass of seething silvery fish trailing along in the wake of the boat. When it was close enough it was transferred to a derrick and winched round to the side of the boat, where it hung suspended in the sea like a gargantuan pearl earring.

On the Mary Louise, Mark said, they'd have brought the net right onto the boat, loosened the cord by hand and released the fish over the deck. Here, a pump was inserted into the net and at the press of a switch the fish were sucked out of the water into containers, which channelled them at a controlled rate down a chute and into the three giant storage tanks. Johnny and Ciaran were regulating the flow and when the tank on the left was only half full they transferred the chute to the right hand tank, counterbalancing the weight and preventing the boat from listing.

Sometimes as they fed the fish into the chutes they'd stop to check the quality of the catch. Reaching into the tumbling cascade they'd pick a fish up and squeeze the convulsing body until either roe or blood exuded from the underside. Roe was a good sign; blood bad, and the ratio of roe to blood determined the price of the catch.

When the net was finally empty the fish filled two-and-a-half tanks. Now it was the Antoinette's turn to shoot and haul and ours simply to help them tow. As we steamed south searching for another shoal, I noticed that the sea had changed. It was darker now and pitted with the crater marks of heavy raindrops. As if from nowhere a swell had risen, billowing against the boat and tossing her about like a plaything.

For a long time nothing happened. The boat rolled rhythmically, accommodating the swell; the coast of Kerry appeared and then faded into the grey blur of the rain. After the excitement of the catch, the wheelhouse was quiet. The skipper was concentrating on the controls; Johnny and Mark and the engineer who had just come in were lost in their own thoughts. An hour must have passed, maybe more. Then the skipper of the Antoinette called to say they'd found a shoal about a mile away. We could see her in the distance as the two skippers spoke: pitching like a see-saw, one minute hidden in a trough, then rising almost vertically, her red bow riding high over the waves.

As quickly as we could we made our way over and Johnny joined Ciaran and one or two others on deck. It was difficult at first to edge the boats close enough to throw the rope: as the Antoinette rose we dipped, increasing the distance between us, and as she lurched one way we veered off in the other direction. But eventually they caught the buoy, and in the now pouring rain, attached it to the winch. The boats pulled apart, increasing speed, and with the net fanning out between them, steamed towards the herring straight ahead.

Soon afterwards the door of the wheelhouse opened and Martin the chef leaned in to tell us breakfast was ready. It was ten-thirty: we had been up since six. The skipper didn't respond; he probably had his brought to the wheelhouse. Mark and I staggered across the wheel-house, down the steps, across the quarter deck and into the galley.

Four or five men were already sitting round the table and as I edged along the bench and sat down one of them speared the last half of a sausage, leant towards it, mouth agape hungrily, and pushed aside his plate. It was smeared with a multi-coloured film of egg yolk, baked beans and tomato ketchup. At the edge there was a pale heap of bacon rind. I realised then that I wasn't hungry. Not many people were. Most were quietly smoking and sipping cups of tea.

Johnny came in, his black hair wet from the rain. 'There's not so many in it this time,' he said, sitting down. The Antoinette must have radioed across with a net-sounder reading.

'I suppose we'll be shooting again so,' said Ciaran.

Suddenly everyone reached for their cups as the boat plummeted. Knives, forks, a plate were shunted, clattering, to the ground.

'Jesus Christ will you stop rolling,' said Ciaran, exasperated.

For an instant the boat balanced, poised at the edge of her trajectory, then with a groan she heaved herself up.

'Whoever built this boat,' said Mark coming back from the toilet, 'Wasn't wasting any space on the jack's. There's hardly room to stand in there.'

'Aye and with legs as long as Ciaran's there's no room to sit either – except with your knees in the air.'

'Shut up Johnny,' said Ciaran warningly.

But Johnny ignored him. 'One day, it must have been a couple years back, we were all sitting here minding our own business when suddenly there was this godalmighty crash. No one could think what had happened. Then the door of the jack's bursts open and Ciaran comes rushing out, trousers round his ankles, shouting for a life jacket. He thought we'd hit the rocks.'

'And what was it?'

'It was the jack's shattering as he sat on it with his legs in the air – that's why we have a steel one now. No point in risking porcelain again.'

The view through the small porthole was grey waves. Slowly it tilted: sea and sky; nothing but sky.

Johnny reached for a slice of bread, buttered it and started eating the sausages Martin had brought him.

Half an hour passed, an hour. Martin cleared the table and washed the dishes. The frying pan full of food that no one could eat remained on the stove, the porridge beside it, untouched. The engineer came in and said that the Antoinette had hauled and the skipper was after another shoal. Once again we were scouring the fishing grounds, up and down, broadside to the swell.

'For fuck's sake will you turn her round,' said Ciaran as the boat dropped heavily. Suddenly there was an ear-splitting boom as a wave cracked over the hull. Patrick had once told me that when you hear that sound on the Mary Louise, without her cover deck, you hide – or are swept overboard. Seconds later the porthole was pelted with water.

For a long time everyone was quiet, concentrating on the motion of the boat. Several people had gone to their bunks, feeling seasick or just passing the time until they were needed. Benny stretched out on an empty seat, head back against the wall, eyes closed, legs loosely crossed so one ancient lace-less trainer rested lightly over the other. For the fourth or fifth time since we'd left port Martin picked up the tomato-stained Irish Press and leafed through it. Then, realising there was nothing he hadn't read, he pushed it aside.

'Don't you have a video player?' said Mark,

remembering how they'd passed time on the Mary Louise.

'We used to,' said Johnny, 'but the skipper was super-stitious and got rid of it. Thought we were watching blue movies.'

Mark reached up to the shelf above the table and switched on the television. The sound of the news blared out, but the picture was lost in interference.

'Must be too far from the coast,' said Johnny, reaching for a cigarette.

Silence followed.

A faint smell of diesel wafted up from the engine room and mixed with the cloying residue of fried food. Johnny's cigarette coiled fresh clouds into the already smoke-filled atmosphere. Suddenly overcome with nausea I left the table and went outside.

It was still raining, but not as heavily as before, and on the windward side of the boat, cold water showered my face, dripping in rivulets down from my chin. In time Mark came out and joined me. Then Johnny passed on his way to the wheelhouse. Soon afterwards, wind-battered and wet, we followed him up.

Most people who were seasick felt worse in the wheel-house; being higher than the rest of the boat it rolled more. But to me it was a relief: spacious, bright, overlooking on three sides the great expanse of the sea. We were heading for home now; the skipper had decided it was too rough to shoot the nets again. In six hours – maybe slightly more because of the headwind – we'd be drifting into port.

The skipper switched on the radio. Interspersed with crackling, silence and snippets of information intelligible only to fishermen and sailors there was news of the weather: a gale warning for Irish coastal waters, winds north to north-westerly, force seven rising gale force eight with gusts up to 80 miles an hour.

I went out onto the small upper deck. A storm watched from a boat is different from a coastal storm. Even the biggest waves, as they approach the shore, are narrow, collapsing in on themselves in a tumult of white water and spray. Here in the open sea the waves were three times broader than the boat, sweeping through the ocean with a force that was relentless but silent. The only white was the occasional crest, the spray and fallback of the breakers on the boat and the churning wake behind. Even the wind was different at sea: quieter, less antagonistic, with nothing in its path for miles around.

In the distance ahead I could see the Antoinette, rising and dipping as she made her slow progress home, her running lights and red hull bright against the grey sea. A seagull suddenly swooped past the deck, sifted the waves for an illusory fish or some debris thrown from the boat, then rose effortlessly with the wind. Another was perched on the railing near the stern, cautiously scanning the deck for herring.

Already the wind had matted my hair with salt-water.

The salt on my lips was tinged with the smell of fish and the sea. It was then that I almost regretted we weren't staying out longer. Ten days, a week, even one more night to play out the boredom, impatience and seasickness and find out what, if anything, was beyond.

When I went back into the wheelhouse Johnny and Ciaran were talking to the skipper about something they'd heard on the radio. A boat had gone down, somewhere to the north, beyond Saint John's Point. It was a crabber, a thirty-five foot half-decker. It wasn't clear from the report what had happened, but it seemed that the boat had been fishing too close to the coast and had run into the rocks. A passing boat had tried to tow her to safety but she was shipping water too fast. The crew, apparently, were all right, but the boat, almost certainly, was lost.

I went over to the open window where I could look out and feel the fresh air, but not be battered by the wind and rain as I was on the deck.

'How's it going?' said Johnny, coming over.

'Fine … I thought you and Ciaran were joking about the storm.'

'We were. We knew that the wind would pick up, but not this much.'

The boat heaved over. Her whole frame seemed to be straining.

'When I first started fishing I was sick every minute of every day. In the end my throat was so sore I had to have my tonsils out. I thought about quitting most of the time, and I probably would have done, but I had a wife and child at home and I needed the money. Two years it took to get over it. More.'

Slowly the hours passed. From time to time I'd go out on deck, and washed over by the wind and rain, I'd lose myself in thought. Then when the cold began to penetrate I'd go back to the warmth of the wheelhouse and stare out of the window. At one point the skipper asked for a cup of coffee to be brought up to the wheelhouse: the rest of us went down to the galley to make our own. As we were drinking it Martin was washing potatoes, someone else whose name I didn't know had discovered the crossword in the Irish Press, and Benny, still sprawled on the bench, was gently snoring.

Back in the wheelhouse the skipper was on the phone to the harbour arranging for the fish to be auctioned. He told us it was almost always the Japanese who bid for the catch: they relish the roe like caviar, and the fillets they eat for breakfast, pickled with soya sauce. It was a standing joke amongst local fishermen that Japanese buyers, testing the freshness and quality of fish, not only slit them open with a knife, but bite into them just like that as they come off the boat.

Gradually it began to get dark. The coastline, obscured by clouds for most of the day, was visible now, defined by lights. Since leaving the fishing grounds we had been steaming for six and a half hours. Eventually the lights of the harbour came into view.

'That's where the sewage comes out,' said Johnny pointing to an expanse of coffee-coloured scum in the mouth of the bay. Seagulls were clamouring round it, scavenging in droves.

In the shelter of the bay the water was calmer and we steamed quickly into the harbour. The Antoinette, which had been ahead of us all the way, was already moored at the pier, and as the skipper skilfully manoeuvred the Orion into the empty berth behind her, some of her crew were waiting by the bollard ready to tie her up when the rope was thrown over.

Within minutes the fisheries officers came on board. There were two of them: one wearing an immaculate cream trench coat, the other more modestly dressed in an anorak. Both of them were business-like, even officious, with their pens and notebooks and disdainful manner.

Every week the herring boats had to be in by Thursday, and the allowable catch for the week was forty tons. Some of the skippers stayed out longer, selling their catches outside the region, often in Norway. Others, the 'big boys', by-passed restrictions with money. But for most of the boats there was no choice but to stick to the rules.

That night, after a single haul there were more fish in the Orion's tanks than the week's quota. But there was no fine: instead she would be tied up for a month until the end of January. That was what most of the crew had expected, and as it was Christmas no one was too bothered. The next time she went out, the roe season would be over, and she'd be fishing spent herring or daps, mainly for the German market, until September, when the spawning started again.

While the skipper was busy with the fisheries officers the rest of us were down in the galley eating. Martin was frying steak, bringing each one, steaming, to the table as soon as it was ready. Everyone was ravenous, having been unable to eat for most of the day. Each man, as his plate was put down in front of him, fell silent, scooping potatoes from the big pan in the middle of the table, slathering them with butter, reaching for ketchup and mustard, and eating.

After the meal there was a long night still ahead. Several other boats had come in just before us, and we were waiting our turn for the fork-lift trucks to unload the catch. Then when the fish were eventually in the auction hall, the boat would have to be cleaned and hosed down and the equipment left ready for the following trip. Some of the crew had gone down to the harbour to stretch their legs and have a look round. The television, now free of interference, was showing a documentary on marine life in the Caribbean, and everyone at the table was watching, their faces reflecting the light.

Another hour dragged by and I too left the boat for a while. As I climbed onto the rail, ready to step across, I couldn't resist glancing down at the sea and once again I almost lost my nerve. But it was easier stepping off the rail onto the solid pier than the other way round. As I landed and walked away, my knees buckled and I staggered, orientated to the rhythm of the sea. It was still raining and under the electric lights the pier looked dark and greasy, with oil and bits of fish offal floating amongst the puddles.

It was a cold night, with gusts of wind whipping in from the sea and buffeting the harbour buildings. I climbed back onto the boat, confident at last. Johnny was pumping the last load of fish out of the tank, and Ciaran was starting to clean up: throwing the spilled herring back into the sea, and hosing off the blue and white scales that clung to the deck like sodden confetti.

Much later, when everything was finished, Johnny, Ciaran, Mark and I were sitting in the Anchor Bar. The fish had been sold, but for less than the crew had hoped: not only had the roe been damaged in the storm, but the herring were not quite in the peak of their spawning. Already the bar was decorated for Christmas, a foretaste of celebrations to come.

'We'll have one more for the road,' said Ciaran, standing up to go the bar.

When he came back with the drinks he said quietly. 'That's one of the guys from the boat that went down. He was picked up out of the water with only a life-jacket.'

I looked across at the man he'd been talking to; he must have been eighteen or nineteen. He was wearing just a pair of jeans and a white shirt open at the throat.

'I'd say they were lucky,' said Ciaran, 'Very lucky.'

MOLLY MAC

Molly Mac was given her name by the children in the Travellers' school where she taught in Dublin. Her real name was Molly McGinley.

'What'll he say when he sees ye tonight?' they asked her one Friday afternoon.

'Oh I don't know. "How are you? How's it goin'?"'

'Ah come on, will he not say, "Me darlin' Molly Mac, you're lookin' gorgeous. You're the most beautiful girl in Ireland"?'

'I doubt it. He'll probably think it, but he's a farmer – the strong and silent type.'

'Then he'll just wrap his big arms round ye and give ye a long deep kiss on the lips.'

'Aye, that sounds more like him …'

Every Friday Molly caught the bus after school and came to see Conor in Donegal. The journey took five-and-a-half hours. Either he'd be waiting when the bus pulled up or they'd have arranged to meet in one or other of the pubs. They'd spend the weekend together in the cottage they rented about a mile from the village, and then on Sunday, Molly would catch the three o'clock bus home.

Molly had lived in Dublin all her life – she spoke with a Dublin accent – but both her parents came from Donegal. Her father was one of twelve children and many a time she'd surprise me by saying that someone I'd come to know independently was her uncle or aunt. When it came to her cousins, I was completely at a loss; one aunt and uncle had fifteen children, another pair had eight. And to add to my confusion many of these cousins lived abroad and appeared only occasionally at Christmas, or for a few weeks in summer.

As a child, Molly had spent the summer holidays with her grandparents in Donegal. It could have been because of those early memories, or it could have been because she was able to trace her ancestry right back to Pádraig McGinley, one of the first names ever recorded in the valley, that Molly felt Donegal was in her blood. Even when her grandparents had died and she'd left home, she still came back regularly, and it was on one such holiday, when she was staying with one or other of her relatives, that she met Conor. They had been together nearly three years.

Then one day Conor told me they had split up. It wasn't that they no longer cared for each other or that one of them had found somebody else, it was just that neither of them could see a future together beyond school holidays and occasional weekends sandwiched between long and gruelling bus rides. Molly liked her job. Teaching jobs in Donegal were few and far between and when they did fall vacant they had usually been spoken for well in advance. There was little else. And Conor had his land and sheep, and because his brothers and sisters lived in England, a responsibility to his mother and uncle, who both lived alone.

After that, I didn't see Molly for nearly two months. She had told me that she and some friends would be staying in a five-bedroom house in Donnybrook while the owners were in America, so I imagined her there, and teaching. Conor went to the pub most evenings, played his electric guitar when he came home until late into the night, and in the daytime he worked. I don't know how much he missed Molly. We didn't often talk about her.

In the summer Molly came back for a week's holiday. She didn't plan to stay with Conor, and the arrangement was that when they saw each other it would be strictly as friends. But nothing worked out as it should have and within days they were as close as ever. One night when we were all in the pub, a man who had known Molly's father and was obviously very fond of her, nudged me and beckoned, 'Come here'. I leaned towards him and, shielding his mouth and my ear so as not to be overheard, he whispered, 'Those two are wild in love.'

And so one week led to another and Molly stayed the summer. She worked on the bog with Conor, turning the cut turf so all sides dried in the sun, then stacking it in loose piles for the wind to blow through; she helped with the hay, raking and tossing it, and gathering it into neat rows for the baler; she went up the hills with him to fetch in the ewes for shearing. Once or twice when the weather was warm the two of them even went swimming together. Molly often swam on her own. She had loved the sea since a recent holiday in Turkey when it was so hot that the sea was the only comfortable place to be. But Conor had always hated it.

One night at about ten o'clock – it was still light outside, hardly even twilight – the two of them came into the pub. It was Friday. Their hair was still damp from the shower and they looked clean and smart and ready for a night on the town. They sat down at the bar and ordered their drinks.

'What were you two at the day?' someone asked them.

'Fishing,' said Molly.

'Catch anything?'

'Aye. A salmon.'

'You were on the river then?'

'No. Down on the rocks.'

Everyone stared. To catch a salmon in the river was rare enough, but to catch one in the sea was almost unheard of.

'Ah, you're having us on.'

Smiles spread tentatively across two or three faces. But then one of the most experienced fishermen in the valley intervened. 'It does happen,' he said. 'They lie in wait at the mouth of the estuary until the tide fills so they can swim upriver to spawn and, very occasionally, they'll bite. 'What size was he, Molly?'

Molly held out her hands about a yard apart, looking from one to the other, adjusting the distance between them.

'Ah, for goodness sake, a buck like that must have given you a rare auld run for your money.' There was admiration in his tone. Many a time that same man would come back from a day on the river saying he'd had the company of a salmon for half an hour or more: he'd played him with every ounce of ingenuity he could muster, reeling him in inch by inch, but in the end 'the bugger skedaddled'. Exhausted, empty-handed, yet somehow satisfied, he'd tried to explain that to a true fisherman it was the contest that counted, the thrill of pitting your own strength and intelligence against those of the fish.

'Was he hard to land, Molly?'

'Nah, not really. Conor helped me.

'He was awkward enough now,' Conor corrected her. On the river they'd probably have used a landing net.

'What lure were you using, Molly?'

'Just a Toby.'

One or two people shook their heads, incredulous.

'Ah, it was good though, wasn't it Conor? We had a couple of steaks before we came out. Beautiful. There's

nothing can beat a fresh salmon straight from the sea –
especially one that you caught yourself.'

Molly was loving this. To watch her, you'd have thought
she had just won the lottery. She was buying drinks all
round, promising salmon steaks, smiling as though her
face had been moulded, and for the benefit of newcomers,
telling the story again and again, sometimes with feigned
modesty sometimes unashamedly bragging.

All through the summer I had the feeling – although
I may have been wrong – that Molly was living on
borrowed time. Her plans hadn't changed; they'd just
been suspended. In September she'd still have to go back
to Dublin, committing herself to the life she had there
and whatever future it offered, without Conor. But in the
meantime she was allowing herself a bit of a fling: late
nights, late mornings; long days outdoors becoming fit
and brown from the work, the walking and swimming;
evenings out with Conor, and a succession of friends
coming to stay from Dublin and all over the country.

One evening at the end of August a group of musicians
from Leitrim were playing in Keany's. A banjo, along
with fiddle, guitar, whistle and flute made familiar tunes
sound like American country and western. Everyone was
enjoying themselves; yahooing appropriately and beating
out the rhythm with fingers and feet and anything else
available. At one point someone lamented the death of

an old man who had been so good on the spoons they virtually 'sang for him'.

Well after midnight when the players had gone home, those left behind were still in the mood for music and one after another people started to sing. First was an elderly man with 'My Wild Irish Rose'. Obviously he had been good at one time, but the high notes were shaky now, his voice grown brittle with age. Everyone was quiet, moved by the sad beauty of the song. When he'd finished a woman launched into 'The Hills of Donegal'. It was a tune everyone knew well and from time to time other people joined in. Then there was silence; the evening was slipping away and, reluctant to let it go, a couple of young men looked round for someone they thought might be willing to sing, but needed encouragement. They focused on Molly. Molly resisted. But when their subsequent attempts on other people similarly failed, they returned to her, cajoling, flattering. In the end she relented.

> Don't get married, girls,
> You'll sign away your life.
> You may start off as a woman
> But you'll end up as the wife.
> You could be a vestal virgin
> Take the veil and be a nun.
> But don't get married, girls,
> For marriage isn't fun.

Oh it's fine when you're romancing and he plays
    the lover's part
You're the roses in his garden, you're the flame
    that warms his heart
And his love will last forever and he'll promise
    you the moon
But just wait until you're married and he'll sing a
    different tune …

So don't get married, girls,
It's very badly paid,
You may start off as a mistress
But you'll end up as the maid.
Be a daring deep-sea diver
Be a polished polyglot
But don't get married, girls
For marriage is a plot.

Have you seen him in the morning with his face
    that looks like death?
He's got dandruff on his pillow and tobacco on his
    breath?
And he wants some reassurance with his cup of
    tea in bed
Cos he's got worries with the mortgage and the
    bald patch on his head.

So don't get married, girls,
Men are all the same,
They just use you when they need you,
You'd do better on the game.
Be a call girl, be a stripper,
Be a hostess, be a whore,
But don't get married, girls, for marriage is a
    bore ...

All the time Molly was singing she hadn't once lifted her eyes from the pint glass in her lap. But she must have felt the penetrating gazes: the shock, the embarrassment.

People were surreptitiously looking at Conor now, wondering what *his* reaction would be, whether he realised that all this reflected on him and was angry or ashamed. But Conor was sitting perfectly calmly at Molly's side, tweaking his long moustache, and meeting their questioning looks with half-smiling brown eyes that were an answer in themselves.

When she had finished, with a little flourish on the last note, a group of middle-aged women cheered: 'Good on you, Molly'. At a quiet table in the corner, a teenage girl, carefully dressed and made up for a date, turned to her boyfriend looking for some kind of reassurance that in ten years' time she wouldn't be cooking, cleaning and rearing children for a bald headed old fart who didn't appreciate her. But the boyfriend, not knowing what to say, shrugged helplessly.

Molly took a sip from her drink.

In time the background noise of the pub resumed and, in a voice that was probably louder than he intended, a sheep farmer from the hills muttered, 'She must be a feminist.'

Molly went back to Dublin the day before her term began, catching the three o'clock bus as usual. But everything had changed. She had applied for a job with a local organisation whose aim was to integrate Down's syndrome children into mainstream education. If she got the job she'd move to Donegal.

The following weekend when she came to see Conor I realised just how much she wanted the job. She told me she was tired of Dublin, tired of the demands on her to be social worker as well as teacher; to help children who were in trouble with the law or whose home-life was in turmoil; to act as some kind of counterpoint to a system that was resolutely biased against Travellers.

In November Conor told me she was one of seven who were going to be interviewed. Soon afterwards I heard that she'd got the job.

At Christmas Molly stepped off the bus grinning like a teenager who had just been told that the boy of her choice was in love with her. She greeted Conor and then the two of them helped the bus driver unload boxes, bags and bin liners full of clothes, books, shoes, kitchen equipment, stacking them up in a heap on the road outside Keany's. She had even persuaded the bus driver to load up three or four cookers and fridges – the kind of appliances that in cities can be acquired for nothing or picked up cheaply, but in the country often have to be bought new. Although she and Conor didn't need them, there'd be plenty of people who did.

In hindsight, Molly told me one evening when Mark and I were having dinner at their cottage, Dublin had been like a sentence from which she'd just been released. Nevertheless, she added, the last few weeks had been fun, with plays and pantomimes and carol singing. On the last day of term there had been a farewell party for her. The Traveller children had given her a good luck card, 'To Molly Mac', with a message from each of them, and teasing her about her new life on the farm, they'd bought her a pop-up picture book entitled, *Farm Animals.*

In January, Molly bought a new white Opel Kadett and started work. The car was necessary for the job, which entailed driving to schools in different parts of the county, teaching Down's syndrome children indi-vidually for several hours a week, and attending meet-ings with parents and teachers. Sometimes she drove as much as seven hundred miles a week. But she said she enjoyed the job, including, for the time being, the travelling: getting to know the countryside, listening to music as she drove.

Inevitably Molly's life had changed from the way it had been in the summer. It wasn't just the job or the car; it was the difference between living from day to day and having a future to build. She and Conor no longer went out every night. In fact they were rarely seen in the pubs, except at weekends. They started to dig and carefully fence-in a vegetable patch, they bought two young milking goats, which they installed in the byre, and soon afterwards a clutch of hens appeared, scrabbling about in the dirt outside the front door.

Although Molly had no grand schemes for self-sufficiency or 'getting back to the land', she wanted to make the most of what they had. Their vegetable patch was amongst the biggest I'd seen. Other people often felt that vegetables were cheap enough to buy and that it was a losing battle to keep out the sheep. Similarly, for the price of a few eggs you could save yourself the disappointment of a fox's nighttime raid. The goats, I think, were Molly's idea. Conor had a sheep-farmer's disdain for the snow-white prima donnas, which had to be pampered and kept indoors. But Molly had her eyes firmly fixed on the years ahead, when they'd be enjoying goat's cheese and selling the surplus to tourists.

Towards Easter, when the weather was getting warmer, the landlord of their cottage offered to install a damp-proof course and re-plaster and paint the walls. Delighted, Molly and Conor moved in with a friend for a couple of weeks. But when the work was finished and the cottage was at last warm, dry and free of mould, the landlord pointed out that, in the holiday season, he could now let it to tourists for considerably more, and doubled the rent. Molly and Conor moved out.

Ideally they told me, they would have bought a house, preferably one with land. But there weren't many for sale, and most of those that were on the market were beyond their means. Five years previously things might have been different. Now they were competing with foreigners looking for second homes. For weeks, the two of them drove round the valley investigating houses they had heard or suspected were empty. Many of these turned out to be holiday homes, occupied albeit for only a few weeks a year. Others that *were* empty had been jointly inherited by a generation of emigrants who still harboured the possibility that one day one or other of them might want to return. A few were on the books of foreign estate agents, who could expect a fortune for a dilapidated cottage with no land, but a clear view of the sea.

In the end they settled for renting a house about four miles from their previous cottage and, by coincidence, next door to where Conor grew up, and where his uncle still lived. It wasn't ideal. Since it had been built, five years previously, it had been used only by tourists and at first it seemed stark and lacking in comfort, but because the landlord was a friend and prepared to forgo the higher summer rents, it was cheap, and for the time being suited them well.

By the beginning of the summer, the house looked unmistakably theirs, with pictures on the walls, and great thickets of busy Lizzies, geraniums and tomato plants. The goats were still too young to milk, but the hens were laying more eggs than the two of them could eat, and the garden was producing a steady supply of vegetables, which they shared with friends and neighbours, some of whom had never seen the likes of spinach or mange-touts.

One day Molly came back from work with a present for Conor: an eleven-month-old black-and-white sheep dog puppy. She had bought it from the father of one of her pupils for a fraction of the usual price for a bitch of her breeding. Everyone who saw the puppy agreed that she looked good: low on the ground, strong legs, widely-spaced, intelligent eyes. But within months, the mere mention of the dog worked like a motor reflex, always and inevitably triggering an argument.

'Oh aye, she's sharp enough. If the kids are playing football, she'll be watching like a hawk, or if a bird flies past, or even a wasp, her eyes'll be glued. But show her a sheep, and you'd be better off with a teddy bear.'

'That's because she's always been tied up out there. If you'd had her out with you every day and worked her right from the start, she'd be a different dog by now.'

'Molly, you've never trained a dog. Either they have it in them or they don't. That one doesn't – or if it ever did, it was too long messing around with kids before we ever set eyes on it.'

Occasionally the arguments ended in laughter. 'We could always call her Peile.'

'Why Peile?'

'It's Irish for football'

But things went from bad to worse. From taking no interest at all in sheep, the dog started running at them, scattering the flock and intimidating the weakest. One day she caught a ewe by the throat, almost throttling it. That was the last time Conor took her out. Then, to their dismay, they discovered she was pregnant. And when the puppies were born she turned vicious so Molly was afraid to go near the oil-drum kennel where she was tethered, even to feed her or to hang out the washing.

In the end they considered destroying her; but Conor wanted to wait. If the puppies were good, there'd be money to be made from future litters.

'I'm not keeping a dog tied up for the rest of its life just to be used as a breeding machine.'

And so they had little choice. One morning, with Molly's consent, Conor took the dog to be put down. But, as luck would have it, they passed a neighbour who reckoned she was a 'fine-looking bitch, with breeding in her', and although he was no longer as young as he had been, he might be able to train her. Molly was delighted; the dog had been given one last chance.

But, the arguments continued. With the mother gone, Molly took pity on the puppies shivering in the cold, and brought them into the house. She put them in a cardboard box by the fire and when they started to whimper, she picked them up and cuddled them.

'Molly, if you want a dog as a pet, that's fine. We'll get a Yorkshire terrier. But if we want a working dog, it'll have to be trained from the start, and this is *not* the way to do it.'

There was, of course, great speculation about whether Molly and Conor would ever get married. A few people thought they'd want to have children and that would be the incentive. But then again, Conor had always been a rebel – in his early twenties he'd looked like Jimi Hendrix with his black Afro and purple velvet flares – and everyone knew, or thought they knew, Molly's views on marriage.

So when the invitations arrived, most people thought they were joking. Not only were they getting married, they were getting married in church. They'd had several long meetings with the priest, who was unusually broad-minded and had in the end agreed to a church ceremony, despite the fact that they had been living together and refused to attend one of the pre-marital courses run by the Church to prepare couples for a Catholic marriage in which there was no possibility of divorce, and the only approved method of contraception was calculated abstinence.

In the weeks that followed, the forthcoming wedding was the talk of the town. A wedding was rare, rarer by far than a funeral, with so many young people living abroad. One old man promised to put another nick in the rafters – a tradition by which each house used to clock up the weddings it saw. Others helpfully informed Conor, who hadn't been to Mass since he was a teenager, that the church was the building with no chimney. And a group of friends, locally and from Dublin, spent hours in the pub and on the telephone, laughing as they discussed what kind of farm animal to give them as a present.

The idea, I think, started with Molly's friends in Dublin, and gained momentum as it spread across the country. But when Conor sensed what was afoot, he was horrified. Sheep and possibly goats, were one thing; but donkeys, pigs, ducks and geese were a different proposition altogether – a responsibility to look after and expensive to feed. And as the wedding approached, he grew more and more convinced that someone would turn up at the church with a sow and a litter of piglets, all with red ribbons tied round their necks.

But by this time the plans were well under way and on the eve of the wedding we all took the two of them on a mystery tour. 'Is it animal, vegetable or mineral?'

Conor asked hopefully. But he knew where the car was going and long before it drew up at his neighbour's byre, he started to wince. Even the friends who had been so looking forward to this moment, were daunted, struggling to maintain the spirit of the occasion, teasing him and passing him a freshly opened bottle of champagne. Molly was braver. But then the whole idea of a farmyard of animals – the goats, the hens, even the dogs – had been hers, not his.

Inside the byre there was a ripe smell of warm manure. Five or six cows tethered along one wall shifted restlessly under the electric lights. Then from a makeshift stall behind the door a small rumpled-looking calf peered out, wild-eyed with fright at this sudden commotion. Molly fell for it immediately. Conor put his face in his hands, complaining that they had nowhere to keep it, that it would cost them a fortune to feed. But when the neighbour, who had bought the calf and been to great lengths to select the best animal on offer, produced proof of her rare and prized Blue Angus pedigree, there was little doubt that Conor was merely acting the part expected of him. More champagne was drunk, photos were taken and the calf was left in peace.

The wedding was on a cold and windswept November afternoon. As three o'clock approached, the church gradually filled with people, silent in thought or prayer, or talking quietly. There was Molly's father; Conor's mother and uncle; Conor's brother and sisters and their families from England; Molly's sisters and a gang of friends who had taken over the Dublin bus the previous day. The ceremony was unlike any church wedding I'd ever been to. There was no Mass, no Holy Communion; Molly was not given away by one man to another – she and Conor walked down the aisle together. Nor did she change her name from Molly McGinley. They made their vows, the priest gave a short sermon stressing the importance in marriage of faithfulness and communication, and in the silence that followed Michael Boyle played a slow air on the fiddle.

Afterwards there was a party at the local hotel and when the meal was over and Conor and the best man had made the customary speeches, everyone insisted that Molly should also say a few words. Molly stood up and, without a moment's hesitation, announced that her speech would be unconventional, a song. Her Dublin women friends joined in the chorus of 'Don't Get Married, Girls'. But on that occasion at least, Molly elicited no sympathy. Conor, sitting beside her, looked like a South American film star, with his black hair and moustache, his white shirt and chestnut suede waistcoat.

The party went on until six in the morning. There was a band and dancing until one, then improvised music with singing and guitars, fiddles and flutes, and finally, when the faint-hearted had gone home, a relaxed roundabout conversation over one last whiskey.

For three more days the celebrations continued. Then in the quiet of the fourth dawn I asked Molly if I could write about her salmon and her song in my book.

'Surely,' she said. 'But about the salmon – there's a bit of a twist to that story.'

'What do you mean?'

'I'll tell you one day in private.'

And she did. She hadn't caught the salmon at all. She'd bought it from a neighbour who had landed it in his nets, from a boat. She'd invented the whole thing, just for the crack. And she still hadn't confessed to anyone.

LEAVING

It was early September. A sheet of low cloud clung over the hills and there was a new bitterness in the wind that lashed at our faces each time we went out. We started to have a fire, first in the evenings, then in the daytime, letting it roar until the back boiler thumped, pumping hot water into the radiators and the whole house was warm. In the village the holiday season was over: Molly had gone back to work; Seamus had tied up his boat for the winter and was back at the fish processing factory; and as the nights closed in local people no longer joined tourists in the bars for long nights of improvised music, choosing instead to stay at home by the fire watching television.

In October Mark got a phone call from a film company he had worked for in England asking him to stand in for a couple of weeks for a cinematographer who was ill.

One day, soon after he'd gone, I wrapped myself up warmly in anorak and walking boots, packed some sandwiches, and set off for a long walk over the cliffs. I stayed out all day losing myself in a world where there was only wind and seabirds and convolutions of foam swirling over the rocks. When I got home tired in the evening, I made myself something to eat then stayed at the table in the window with the lights off so I could look out over the bay and watch the reflection of the moon bobbing over the waves.

The last time I saw my father was in Bloomsbury. We'd had lunch in a pub before he went to his conference at the university. I remember him walking away, an unmistakably Irish figure, tall, elegant in his suit, hurrying slightly as we'd taken too long saying goodbye.

A cloud passed over the moon, dulling its glow on the sea.

Sometimes I found him in dreams: he was older now, wearing an overcoat, looking for something, maybe lost. But the memories were starting to fade.

When I met Mark at the airport he seemed exhilarated – pleased to be back but also excited by the film he'd been making, by being part of a team that was doing the work he loved. He told me about old friends he'd met up with, a concert he'd been to, the crazy pace of life in the city. Gradually over the next week, it became clear that during our time apart our thoughts had arrived at a similar place.

When we told Molly and Conor, our closest friends, that we were thinking of leaving, they both said they'd miss us and for a moment we hesitated. But when Molly suggested we have a going-away party at Wattie's we all became animated and suddenly the plan had a momentum all of its own. We arranged a date. Molly and Conor kindly said they'd do the cooking if we provided the drinks. It would be a perfect way to say goodbye to our friends, and thank them.

The party was on a clear night at the end of November. Mark and I had spent all day preparing the cottage and it looked beautiful with candles and fairy lights and a bright fire in the grate. We had hung a hurricane lamp outside the front door to help people find their way up the grassy track and another by the turn off from the road. Nearly all our friends came: Johnny and Ciaran from the trawlers, Patrick and his wife Annie, Seamus and Diarmaid who had taken me lobster fishing. Even the priest turned up for a while. Wattie's was throbbing with laughter and fun.

We spent the following two weeks cleaning the house, packing and saying goodbye to people who hadn't come to the party: Margaret, who lived in another village and could hardly believe we were leaving; Brid McGahern, who owned Wattie's, and whose husband Frank had recently passed away; the fishermen from Killybegs who'd been on the Mary Louise with Mark.

Eventually we loaded the car and drove slowly out of the village.

Mark has often told me since that those years in Donegal were the happiest time of his life. As for me, the west of

Ireland will probably always be the place that resonates most deeply with me. The sound of sheep bleating on isolated hillsides; the smell of turf fires; splashes of sun on the horizon as a shower bursts over the sea: all linked in my heart with my father.

But the time had come to move on.

GLOSSARY

buillig	submerged rock
byan	wrasse
Carraig na Broigheall	Cormorant Rock
Chlock Mhor, An	The Big Boulder
Coirnéal, An	The Corner
galach	string of fish
glasán	coalfish
Gub, The	The Point
Leic na Magach	Pollack Rock
ludar	big fish
maorach	whelk or limpet soup
Ramatia	fishing point: the meaning of the name, if there was one, has been lost
scra	top layer of bog including plants and roots
seabhac cac an faoileós	birds that eat waste: fulmars
sleán	turf spade
Tearáil, The	fishing point: the meaning of the name, if there was one, has been lost

APPENDIX

Don't Get Married, Girls
Leon Rosselson

Don't get married, girls,
You'll sign away your life.
You may start off as a woman
But you'll end up as the wife.
You could be a vestal virgin
Take the veil and be a nun.
But don't get married, girls,
For marriage isn't fun

Oh it's fine when you're romancing and he plays a
    lover's part
You're the roses in his garden, you're the flame
    that warms his heart
And his love will last forever and he'll promise
    you the moon
But just wait until you're wedded and he'll sing a
    different tune.

You're his tapioca pudding, you're the dumplings
    in his stew
And he'll soon begin to wonder what he ever saw
    in you.
Still he takes without complaining all the dishes
    you provide
But you see he has to have his bit of jam tart on
    the side.

So don't get married, girls,
It's very badly paid,
You many start off as the mistress
But you'll end up as the maid.
Be a daring deep-sea diver
Be a polished polyglot
But don't get married, girls,
For marriage is a plot.

Have you seen him in the morning with a face that
    looks like death?
He's got dandruff on his pillow and tobacco on his
    breath
And he wants some reassurance with his cup of
    tea in bed
Cos he's got worries with the mortgage and the
    bald patch on his head.

And he's sure that you're his mother, lays his head
    upon your breast
So you try to boost his ego, iron his shirt and
    warm his vest,
Then you get him off to work, the mighty hunter
    is restored
And he leaves you there with nothing but the
    dreams you can't afford.

So don't get married, girls,
Men are all the same,
They just use you when they need you,
You'd do better on the game.
Be a call-girl, be a stripper,
Be a hostess, be a whore,
But don't get married, girls,
For marriage is a bore.

When he comes home in the evening, he can
    hardly spare a look
All he says is 'What's for dinner?' after all you're
    just the cook.
But when he takes you to a party, he eyes you with
    a frown
And you know you've got to look your best, you
    mustn't let him down.

Then he'll clutch you with that 'Look what I've
    got' sparkle in his eyes
Like he's entered for a raffle and he's won you for
    the prize.
But when the party's over, you'll be slogging
    through the sludge
Half the time a decoration and other half a
    drudge.

So don't get married
It'll drive you round the bend
It's the lane without a turning
It's the end without an end.
Change your lover every Friday
Take up tennis, be a nurse
But don't get married, girls,
For marriage is a curse.

Then you get him off to work, the mighty hunter
    is restored
And he leaves you there with nothing but the
    dreams you can't afford.

ACKNOWLEDGMENTS

I will always be grateful to the people who appear in the book not only for all they taught me about Donegal but for their warmth, hospitality, friendship and terrific sense of fun. I am equally grateful to Mark Chamberlain, my first husband, for living in Donegal with me; without his warm exuberance and easily won friendships, Gathering Carrageen would be a very different book.

My thanks are also due to everyone at Sandstone Press, particularly Moira Forsyth, who with kindness, patience and an expert critical eye, guided me through the final stages of shaping the book. Thanks, too, to the K. Blundell Trust for a research grant, which helped prolong my stay in Ireland.

The support and encouragement of friends, family and colleagues during the long years of creating the book has been indispensible to me. In particular I would like to thank Myra Connell, who read each chapter as I wrote it and whose comments were always helpful and supportive,

George and Brenda Dick, whose cottage in Donegal I stayed in as a child, Caroline Shearing, their daughter, Ursula Monn, Barnaby Rogerson, Rose Baring, Richard Skinner, Ingrid Price-Gschössl, Kieran and Laurence Connell, Benji and Jacob Mitchell and of course, Adrian Mitchell – friend, companion, and husband.

Finally, my thanks are due to Leon Rosselson for permission to quote from his wonderful song, 'Don't get married, girls', which is reproduced in full as an appendix.